The Westerly

THE
WESTERLY
WANDERER

A BRIEF PORTRAIT OF
A.E.HOUSMAN
AUTHOR OF
A SHROPSHIRE LAD
1896—1996

❧❧❧

JEREMY BOURNE

THE HOUSMAN SOCIETY

First published in Great Britain in 1996
by The Housman Society,
Bromsgrove, Worcestershire B60 2LA

ISBN 0 904579 06 9
British Library Cataloguing-in-Publication Data
A catalogue record for this book is available from the
British Library

Designed and produced by Geoff Green
at Silent Books Ltd, Swavesey, Cambridge CB4 5QG
Typeset in Ehrhardt
Printed in Great Britain by
Ebenezer Baylis and Son Limited
The Trinity Press, Worcester

Cover illustration
From an original painting by Don Davidson

for Ann with love

❧❧❧

Preface

THIS portrait study of A. E. Housman is not an exhaustive biography. It is intended for the newcomer to Housman's poetry, the general reader who has heard of him, who knows of one or two or of his more famous poems, and who would like to explore a little of the poet's personality and inspiration without plunging into a lengthy, academic biography. For the serious student of Housman, full and academic biographies already exist, covering both his poetic inspiration and his quite separate vocation as a scholar. I must acknowledge my own debt to the more recent authors of these: Richard Perceval Graves, Norman Page, Henry Maas, Keith Jebb, and to those two most thorough and scholarly Housman archivists, P. G. Naiditch and Joe Hunt. A new edition of Housman's Complete Poems is shortly to be published by Archie Burnett. A bibliography appears at the end of this book. For present purposes, however, I have confined myself to direct quotations only, from Housman's own letters and poems, and from the writings of his brother Laurence and sister Kate.

I must thank a number of people who have given me a great deal of help. Michael and Gerald Symons, Housman's great-nephews, have given kind permission to quote a good deal of family material, and to use family photographs some of which have not previously been published. Cicely Symons, daughter-in-law of Housman's sister Kate, has given to the Housman Society ownership of the copyright in her mother-in-law's writings. Random House U. K. Ltd. and the Society of Authors, owners of copyright in the works of Laurence Housman and A. E. Housman respectively, have guided us through the changes in copyright law, and I am grateful for their permission to quote. Members of the committee of the Housman Society, and especially Jim

Page, the Chairman, who helped me to select the illustrations, and Jennie McGregor Smith, the Secretary, have given encouragement and made suggestions in countless ways. Patrick Gillibrand, once of Imperial Airways, and Don Upward of the Hall of Aviation, Southampton, have given pictures and invaluable information about Housman's cross-channel flights. We also acknowledge the great kindness of the celebrated restaurant *La Tour d'Argent*, in providing us with photographs. Robin Shaw and Roy Birch have gone through my manuscript with great care and suggested many improvements - but any errors that remain are entirely my own. Lastly, my wife Ann has not only gone through the manuscript but has also pointed out many areas where my more pedantic turn of mind might have discouraged the everyday reader for whom this book has been written. To all of these people I am sincerely grateful.

When A. E. Housman published *A Shropshire Lad* in 1896, initially at his own expense, he could hardly have foreseen that his slim volume of wistful, tender, ironic and sometimes brutal verses, with their folksong rhythm and piping rhymes, was to become one of the most popular cycles ever written. For *A Shropshire Lad* is one of the few collections that has remained in print, and available in bookshops, for one hundred years without interruption. The Housman Society have celebrated this event with a number of new commissions, of which this is one. It is their hope and mine that a brief portrait such as this will make the poems more enjoyable to a wider readership. More especially, we hope it will lead to a new understanding of their learned, complex, human, secretive and endearingly reticent author.

ભાજભાજ

Lovers, soldiers, countrymen, death

W E discovered A. E. Housman when we were students. Those years between eighteen and twenty-two always bring disturbing new perceptions about happiness and grief, beauty and ugliness, war and peace, passion and death. Housman himself learned them at that age, and suffered long for them.In this my friends and I were no exception; we read, recited and listened to his simple verses, and we realised what lay behind the even rhythms, the methodical rhymes, the pretty, pastoral scenes and the self-concsiously aching sentiment. Housman, we felt, knew about falling in love, about rejection, frustration, danger. He knew how to place those feelings within a setting of wonderful landscape, a countryside that was forever England. For a year or two, we were his devoted admirers. There were perhaps four or five reasons why he struck a chord with us: In the first place, some of us were in love. As often as not, the object of our love was remote; real enough across a lecture theatre or walking by the river, but as to true character, nothing more than a figment of the imagination. Many of our friends were more in love with love than seriously in pursuit of the pleasures of the flesh. A few, in those days before equal educational rights for girls, had real girlfriends to take to college dances; but even they were misunderstood, hopelessly idealised, and expected to play a part they only dimly appreciated. So Housman's nostalgic, yearning and jealous lovers exactly suited our mood, and we learnt the relevant poems by heart. Number XIII from "A Shropshire Lad" was one of the most popular:

When I was one-and-twenty
  I heard a wise man say,
"Give crowns and pounds and guineas
  But not your heart away;
Give pearls away and rubies
  But keep your fancy free."
But I was one-and-twenty,
  No use to talk to me.
When I was one-and-twenty
  I heard him say again,
"The heart out of the bosom
  Was never given in vain;
'Tis paid with sighs a-plenty
  And sold for endless rue."
And I am two-and-twenty,
  And oh, 'tis true, 'tis true.

A second reason had to do with war. Many of us in those days had served unwillingly in the armed forces; like those earlier Housman dreamers, in the trenches of the First World War or in the Burmese jungle during the Second, we had known the fear of lying low under fire; in Cyprus perhaps, in Suez, in Crossmaglen. We had suffered the soldier's classic trauma: war is two-thirds intense boredom to one-third intense fear. For these, too, Housman's raw recruits, marching to war with drums beating, colours flying and hearts broken, had a poignant appeal:

The Recruit

Leave your home behind, lad,
  And reach your friends your hand,
And go, and luck go with you
  While Ludlow tower shall stand.

Oh, come you home of Sunday
  When Ludlow streets are still
And Ludlow bells are calling
  To farm and lane and mill,

Or come you home of Monday
 When Ludlow market hums
And Ludlow chimes are playing
"The conquering hero comes,"

Come you home a hero,
 Or come not home at all,
The lads you leave will mind you
 Till Ludlow tower shall fall.

And you will list the bugle
 That blows in lands of morn,
And make the foes of England
 Be sorry you were born.

And you till trump of doomsday
 On lands of morn may lie,
And make the hearts of comrades
 Be heavy where you die.

Leave your home behind you,
 Your friends by field and town
Oh, town and field will mind you
 Till Ludlow tower is down.

This, Number III in "A Shropshire Lad", seemed to combine as neatly as anything by Rudyard Kipling the outward, public glory of the call to arms with its inward misery, physical pain and likelihood of brutal and inglorious death. Indeed, death was a key factor in Housman's ensemble of emotions. Death provided a third reason for the fascination he exerted upon us. It played a leading part in the nostalgia, the pit-of-the-stomach masochism which he knew so well how to exploit, and from which he too was a sufferer. The fear of death was not so much the physical hurt or the injustice, but rather more the terror of leaving so much behind – unconsummated love, the views of home, merry companionship. The creatures of Housman's Shropshire die in dramatic fashion, by shooting, stabbing, mysterious disease and hanging; their bodies are left to rattle in chains on windswept moors or rot bleeding in barley fields. In two of the poems, "Is My Team Ploughing?" and "The True Lover", the heartsick young man is already dead and speaks from beyond the grave, in order to pursue his fickle sweetheart. In the former poem, he is long buried beneath the sod as he speaks, but in the latter he creeps into the poor girl's bed, like some ethereal vampire, to take her in his arms while the blood is still pouring from the neck wound where he has cut his own throat for love.

There was a yet a fourth theme, a more visibly charming one, that drew us to "A Shropshire Lad." Several of the friends I knew as a student had their roots in the land of Severn Vale; Worcestershire, the North Cotswolds or the South Shropshire borders. We knew from our boyhood the great sweep of that wide plain, with its spacious, cloud-dappled, windy skies and its circle of distant hills; the Cotswold scarp and Bredon Hill to the South; the Malverns, the faraway line of the Black Mountains and the Clees to the West; the Wrekin, Wenlock Edge and the Long Mynd to the North-West, and the lesser boundary of the Clent and Lickey Hills to the North. This world, encompassing much of the best in traditional English agricultural landscape, was for us the world of girlfriends left behind, of childhood rambles, of homesickness. Before ever we owned a volume of Housman's verse, we had a

Ludlow and the Clee Hills

record of Butterworth's orchestral rhapsody, "A Shropshire Lad", and the sleeve of this record was ornamented with a photograph of Severn Vale from Broadway Hill. It showed Bredon in the centre ground and the thin, wavy line of the Malverns on the horizon. It epitomised for me as a young man all the enchantment of Housman country, that wonderful, westward-looking world where the poet must have wandered. As an old man, I live today a mere three miles from that viewpoint, and find it as magical as ever I did when a student.

> Into my heart an air that kills
>   From yon far country blows:
> What are those blue remembered hills,
>   What spires, what farms are those?
>
> That is the land of lost content.
>   I see it shining plain,
> The happy highways where I went
>   And cannot come again.

This poem, usually known as "A Far Country" but to Housman himself simply Number XV, provided the title for one of Nevil Shute's bestselling romantic novels of the nineteen-fifties. For Nevil Shute was himself a Shropshire schoolboy. Another best–selling author, P. D. James, has recalled the profound effect upon her of having to learn Housman's poems when a schoolgirl. Colin Dexter has created a Housman enthusiast in his romantically-inclined detective, Inspector Morse. All of these felt the magnetism of Housman's lovers and soldiers, countrymen and dead.

Long before our student discovery of "A Shropshire Lad", I suppose, many of us must have been set as homework the learning of "something by Housman." Like as not, it was "Loveliest of trees, the cherry now…" But whether this meant much to most children - with its injunction to enjoy beauty while you can because life is, alas, only too short – I rather doubt. That sort of introduction to Housman was scarcely a discovery.

In my own case, the earliest moment when I can positively recall that what I was listening to was by Housman, and was truly memorable, occurred in a school music competition. A young man who had been a cathedral treble won the competition by singing, in a piping, newly-fledged tenor, Graham Peel's famous, drawing-room-ballad setting of "In Summertime on Bredon".

For to countryman - lovers of Housman's western world, the music that he inspired is a key factor. It is strange to record that A. E. Housman himself was not particularly endowed with musical sense. To those inspired composers who sought permission to set his work - and there were very many of them - he was rather stand-offish. When Vaughan Williams actually left out two verses of "Is my team ploughing", and weak verses too, Housman was incensed. "How would he like it," Housman wrote, "if I were to leave out two bars of his music?" Nevertheless, the poems are saturated with music, and music of a peculiarly English kind. It is the music of soft skies and fields, of gentle, lonely hills, wind-blown woods and hedgerows, of quiet, trout-filled brooks and distant birdsong. Above all, it is wholly underpinned by the rhythms and rhymes of English pastoral folksong. These are not odes and elegies, nor sonnets, rondeaux and ballades; these are outwardly the poems of simple countrymen and countrywomen, remorselessly catchy in their brief, repetitious metre and never-failing rhyming couplets. You do not find many parallels in the great English Romantics. There is just a whisper of it in works like Keats' "Meg Merrilies" or Wordsworth's "She dwelt among untrodden ways" or "Daffodils". But you could not say with any confidence that Housman sought inspiration from the English Romantics. He did not admit it. He did admit to being influenced by Shakespeare - of course. With "Come Away, Death" and "When that I was...", with "Under the greenwood tree" and "It was a lover and his lass", and especially with "Fear no more the heat of the sun", from Cymbeline, you can detect something of the folksong tradition that Housman felt.

He confessed to being influenced by the Scottish Border ballads; there is a quaint minstrelsy in some poems, rather like the rhythm of:

"Oh, young Lochinvar has come out of the West,
Through all the wide border his steed is the best..."

More oddly, Housman tells us that he was influenced by the German

Shropshire Countryside from Abdon

late Romantic poet Heinrich Heine. Oddly, I suppose, because to us today after two World Wars and a century of commercial and imperial rivalry, English readers do not feel much affinity with German poetry. But it must be remembered that when Housman was young, relations with Germany were of the closest. As G. K. Chesterton put it, "A cousin germane was the same as a German cousin." Prince Albert was still alive when Housman was born. A German governess was absolutely the most respectable person to whom one's children's education might be entrusted, as Housman found when he went to stay at Woodchester.

A study of Heine reveals the precise character of folksong-derived lyric poetry; exactly the rhymes and rhythms that Housman loved. And most important, it was that lyrical, whimsical, nostalgic, ironically yearning and yet cynical poetry that inspired the greatest composers of nineteenth-century Romanticism. When you have listened to Schumann's song cycle based on Heine's poems, "Dichterliebe" (The Love of a Poet), or Schubert's on Wilhelm Müller's poetry, "Winterreise" and "Die Schöne Müllerin", then you begin to understand only too clearly why the leading composers of the English Edwardian revival longed to set to music Housman's "Shropshire

Lad". The list includes Vaughan Williams, Ireland, Butterworth, Somervell, E.J.Moeran, Peel, Orr, Gibbs, Gurney and Bax - a pantheon of English twentieth century song.

These, then, were the special features of the appeal that A. E. Housman held for us: the restless longing of the frustrated or jealous lover; the dreaded parting, the homesickness, the fear of the new recruit; the bewitching Western views of the rolling countryside beyond the Severn; the dread of death - those intimations of mortality which we all must face but which come too soon when the sufferer is young and unfulfilled; and lastly the unforgettable, uniquely musical and folksy metre and wordplay of those deceptively simple lyric verses. It was easy to believe that soldiers on both sides in the two World Wars carried their copies of "A Shropshire Lad" in their haversacks, in those tiny, slim, red-backed editions published by Grant Richards from the turn of the century.

But we grew out of Housman. The appeal was for a few irresponsible years only. Soon one began to perceive other things in the man. For was not Housman himself a homosexual? A covert one, indeed, who never allowed his feelings to show publicly, unlike his contemporary Oscar Wilde; nor was he a pederast, for the men he loved were of his own age. Nevertheless it did not suit the lovers among us to follow his work any further. This was a man whose poems use the words "lad" or "lads" sixty-eight times in one slim volume. His lads have a monopoly of all sentiment, all grace and attraction; but his girls are only cardboard figures, who exist to spurn, ignore and betray, but have no real personality of their own.

Furthermore, it transpired that the poet himself was by no means a romantic Byron or Browning, no rebel like Swinburne or Wilde, but a straitlaced scholar and academic, a Cambridge professor of Latin, an authority on the driest of all Latin poets, and a notoriously dull lecturer and cold social mixer. This was not the man for young people of imagination and wit.

Housman did not die until 1936, so he knew both the Boer War and the First World War. But apart from one particular event during the former, it was apparently not those wars that moved him. He seemed strangely undisturbed by the miserable existence in the trenches suffered by a thousand of his admirers. Before 1896, the raw recruits of "A Shropshire Lad", mustering in their red coats and gold braid, were perhaps on their way to die in the Second Afghan War or the occupation of Ashanti, the conquest of Zululand or the annexation of Somaliland - mere empire-building adventures rather than noble causes. Certainly Housman himself never served as a soldier.

There was a more surprising discovery than these, however: it seemed doubtful that Housman had actually been to many of the places that he describes with such apparent accuracy. Did he simply take the names from a map? Why do his letters make so little mention of actual journeys into Shropshire? At a learned meeting of Housman enthusiasts, I once naively asked, "How did A. E. H. actually get to all these hills and villages which he describes?" There was a surprised silence. Then, as if to a child who does not know the facts of life but who has asked, in polite society, a dangerous question about the birds and the bees, someone mumbled, "Perhaps he went by train. There were a lot more branch lines before Beeching."

Certainly Housman knew and loved Ludlow. The salary of a professor would have allowed him to hire a pony and trap at any station along the Ludlow line to Shrewsbury, and explore wherever his fancy took him. But some of the places which he appears to describe from personal acquaintance were surely seen only from a distance. That seemed to us improper. Then there was the tripping verse; was it really so catchy? Did one not easily tire of it? Some of us tried mockingly to produce home-made Housman - ironically toying with his own themes. It is not hard to do. "With rue my heart is laden, Tiddly-tiddly-pom, And many a rose-lipt maiden, Tiddly-pom-pom-pom." A little trite, a little maudlin, a little shallow, too Victorian by half. And we passed on, to W. B. Yeats, to Wilfred Owen, to T. S. Eliot, and eventually to Charles Causley, Seamus Heaney and Philip Larkin.

But with maturity, one is strangely drawn to Housman the man. In the end, there comes a third stage in our relationship with the secret protagonist of "A Shropshire Lad". There is a certain enigma about this odd, aloof, private, brave, brilliantly clever and quietly dignified academic. He suffered much, and in ways other than those recorded in his poems. He wrote a great deal, far more than "A Shropshire Lad",

Alfred aged 18

but kept so much of what he wrote private and locked away. It was too heartfelt, or else in his opinion not good enough, to allow it to fall into the wrong hands.

Next, there was the astonishing fact that this man, who had failed his university final exams and departed in disgrace, became half-way through his career the Kennedy Professor of Latin at Cambridge; no ordinary student could have made such a brave and hard-fought comeback. Such courage, such ability, needed looking into. Many of those who criticised his rudeness and detachment were themselves too shallow and too glossy to make deep and sincere relationships, whereas Housman numbered among his friends some of the most creative and thoughtful in the land. His brothers and sisters held him in love and respect, and he made them the foremost of his personal responsibilities.

As we came to understand the strangeness of Housman the man, to form in our maturity a more balanced judgement, we began also to read more into those verses we used to love. We came back to Housman, back to "A Shropshire Lad" and to that wistful wanderer in the West. We began in the end to love those poems as much as ever we did in youth, when our emotions were wilder but our critical faculties less controlled. This eccentric, enigmatic but extremely eminent man could write poetry of the most enduring appeal; and yet, unlike so many enduring poets, he revealed only a fraction of his true self in his verse. We may never entirely understand that true self. But today, when our view of love, nature and death has become far removed from that of Housman's time, his true self seems more intriguing than ever.

CHAPTER ONE

May all my boys be like him

THE best place to begin a portrait of a poet is at the site of his original inspiration. In Housman's case, curiously, this is to be found by the M5 Motorway. Due West of the modern town of Bromsgrove, the northbound traveller comes to the slip-roads of the M5 and M42 inter-section, immediately to the West of which lies a small, round, green hill with a black and white television mast on its summit. It is scarcely even a hill worth the name - rather more a piece of undulating down-land ringed with a necklace of redbrick, nineteenth-century farms and barns. This spot is becoming known today as "Housman's Hill". But to the Housman children in the 1860's and 1870's it was known as "Mount Pisgah", after the hill in the Book of Deuteronomy from which Moses glimpsed the Promised Land.

The view from the top is extensive. To the east lies Bromsgrove, in a bowl of hills, with the tall, sharp spire of St John's Church on a mound. But to the West, all is far more romantic and mysterious. The ground drops away first into the wooded combes of Dodford, to rise again to a long, elevated, forested height; the Randan Woods, which border the Chaddesley Wood National Nature Reserve. Above that - far, far away on the western horizon, and unforgettable when the sun is sinking - lie the Shropshire Hills, Titterstone Clee, Brown Clee and the Welsh Border country.

It is only a short climb from the Fockbury farms below, and here the young Alfred Housman would climb of an evening, to gaze into the west. This was his view of the Promised Land, the Land of Lost Content. It was a view he never forgot, and which he continued to refer to in his letters more than sixty years later. That was the westerly world into which, during the most creative years of his early manhood, he would wander in his memory.

He was born on the 26th March 1859. His father, Edward Housman, was a solicitor in Bromsgrove, then a small North Worcestershire market town. It had a long, quietly dignified, redbrick, Georgian High Street lying along the main Birmingham to Bristol road, with a scatter of side alleys and greens. It was encircled by a wide, pastoral, wooded region of outlying, deeply rural parishes. The main trade of the town was nailmaking, and that of the country areas perry cider. Housman would scarcely recognise the booming commuter town of today, and would be astonished by the television mast and the sinuous plait of motorways beside his birthplace – though he was in his later years remarkably open-minded about modern inventions. He might well have approved of the National Nature Reserve.

But Bromsgrove then was hardly a prosperous centre, and Edward was not a prosperous solicitor. He was, indeed, a somewhat incompetent lawyer, and an indulgent but far from competent parent. Alfred's mother, Sarah, the daughter of the Reverend John Williams, Rector of Woodchester near Stroud, was a more gifted person. Her father was an Oxford-educated classicist, poet and scholar, and she inherited his ability to write clever verse, as well as his taste for High-Church Anglicanism. All Alfred's more endearing and literary characteristics seem to have come from his mother and her family – not least his steadfastness in adversity. Alfred was the eldest in a large family. He was followed by Robert in 1860, Clemence in 1861, Katharine in 1862, Basil in 1864, Laurence in 1865 and Herbert in 1868. Clemence and Laurence became well-known in their own right, she as an artist and campaigner for women's rights and world peace, he as a playwright, poet and fellow campaigner for his eldest sister. A. E. H. seems seldom to have corresponded with Clemence, and theirs was the least close relationship. But Laurence he regarded as a literary protégé, and to him he eventually entrusted the editing, after his death, of his own poetic works and letters.

Robert and Basil both died before their elder brother. Robert's memorial at Smallcombe, near Bath, bears an inscription chosen by

Sarah Jane Williams, Alfred's mother

A. E. H. himself. Basil had a quiet career as a doctor, becoming med-
ical officer for Worcestershire. He and his wife Jeannie kept a simple
and intellectually modest home at Tardebigge, on the other side of
Bromsgrove. But it was there that A. E. H. felt most relaxed and "at
home" in his latter days.

A. E. H.'s youngest brother, George Herbert – but he was always
known as Herbert – had been intended for a professional career, but

chose instead to enlist in the King's Royal Rifles. At the outbeak of the Boer War he was a sergeant, and his death in action in 1901 was a sad blow to Alfred, and the source of two of the most beautiful poems.

With Kate, lastly, he shared the most balanced relationship. She was, like her mother, a woman of great inward strength and resource, with a creative and outgoing personality. She married E. W .Symons, a master at Bromsgrove School, who became Headmaster of King Edward's School at Bath. She was the only one of all the Housman children to have children of her own. Her letters to and from A. E. H. are lengthy, charming, and full of absorbing detail about their personal interests.

Alfred was born in Valley House, Fockbury, the hamlet at the foot of "Housman's Hill", in the parish of Catshill where his paternal grandfather, Reverend Thomas Housman, was vicar. A. E. H. is commemorated at Christ Church, Catshill.

Shortly after Alfred's birth, however, Edward Housman moved into central Bromsgrove. The house which he and Sarah now took over, with the baby Alfred, and where the other six children were born, was an improvement. Perry Hall was an elegant manor in Strawberry Hill Gothic style, just across the road from Bromsgrove's large and recently restored parish church. Today Perry Hall is a three-star hotel and much extended and altered, but still proud of its Housman associations.

The house then had a rambling garden and easy access to such delights as Bromsgrove High Street could offer. Just around the corner, opposite today's market, was the old Shoulder of Mutton Inn, which for Edward was a major convenience. Bromsgrove legend has it that outside the inn was a tin penthouse roof, on to which Edward would throw loudly rattling stones in order to warn the servants at home that he was about to return for dinner, generally the worse for drink. It was, indeed, drink that was Edward's ruin. It was the cause of the disaffection later in life between himself and Alfred, and of his somewhat dishonest financial disasters.

For the children, Perry Hall and its garden was a delight. In his autobiography "The Unexpected Years", A. E. H.'s brother Laurence writes:

Alfred was our leader, and - in a very quarrelsome family - the only one with whom we never quarrelled.

Alfred took very seriously his responsibilities as the eldest, an attitude which lasted all his life. It was Alfred who thought up the imaginative games and directed operations.

> Alfred,the eldest of us and always our leader, invented three new instruments of war - the Bath Bridge, the Martin Luther, and the Flying Torpedo; outwardly quite homely objects of garden use, but imaginatively endowed with terrific powers of destruction. The Bath Bridge, a mere drainpipe to look at, was designed to swallow lighted tallow candles at one end and send them rushing out in fire at the other....The Martin Luther was a species of Gatling gun that never gattled, being nothing more than a semi-circle of wood, with a groundstake, for running bird lines; the Flying Torpedo was a stump of wood which he threw. But if they failed to do much execution, the names made us happy; for Alfred was always able to make us believe that his word—inventions had a meaning, and that the meaning was good.

One other place apart from Bromsgrove was to play a formative role in Housman's childhood: Woodchester is a scattered but attractive Cotswold village about two miles south of Stroud, above the road to Bath. It spreads across a steep hillside within a deep combe. Above it lies a pleasant open common on a bluff, with a splendid view across the Severn to Monmouth and Wales. Its chief claim to fame has been the existence, in the old churchyard, of an important Roman villa, containing one of the finest tessellated pavements north of the Alps. But nowadays this is covered with layers of protective sheets, sand and turf. On a visit in adult life, Professor Housman found himself unwillingly engaged to give guided talks to visitors who had come to see the pavement when uncovered.

Woodchester House, a tall and elegant Georgian manor, well-hidden in the woodland of its own grounds, had been the home of Alfred's great-uncle William Housman. Of William's eight children, one - his daughter Lucy - played a very major part in Alfred's life. She it was

Alfred and Robert with their guns

who introduced her friend Sarah Williams, daughter of the Rector of Woodchester, to her cousin Edward Housman of Bromsgrove. There was certainly an element of matchmaking in this, and Lucy felt some responsibility for Sarah and her children, as we shall see.

When William Housman left Woodchester House, it was acquired by Edward Wise, a well-to-do wool manufacturer. He and his family became close friends of the Woodchester Housmans, and especially of the Williams. Thus it was that the young Alfred, who came for a series of holidays to Woodchester, was taken into the home of the Wise family and there made friends for the rest of his life. They must have done him a power of good. His own father was indulgent but neglectful; his mother, with whom he had a particularly creative relationship, was nevertheless constantly in childbed, because little brothers and sisters followed in quick succession; and Alfred suffered the usual fate of the eldest child in a large family – he was expected to grow up too fast and too soon.

But at Woodchester it was different. Amongst the Wise children, he was the youngest, and must certainly have benefitted from the extra loving attention. Many years later he took his sister Kate up from Bath to see these haunts of his childhood, and she tells the following story, which illustrates both his imagination and his adventurous spirit:

> I was shown a spot where he might have made an early ending to his life. When quite a small boy he convinced himself that it would be perfectly safe to jump off the roof of the house if he held on to an open umbrella to float him gently down. He was discovered with a ladder and an umbrella just in time to frustrate the experiment.

The three Wise children had a German governess, Sophie Becker, fourteen years older then Alfred, and an educated woman who greatly influenced his thinking. I could not say for sure that it was she who introduced Alfred to Heinrich Heine's poetry, but given the tastes of German mid-nineteenth century society governesses, it seems likely. A. E. H. corresponded with Sophie all his life. Before the First World War, the Wises lost a good deal of their wealth and Sophie was forced to leave their employ. She returned to Germany, but the correspondence with Alfred continued until her death in 1933, only a few years before his own.

At Woodchester the young Alfred heard the news of the first major disaster to shape the course of his life. By the time he was eleven years old, his mother Sarah was seriously ill. She seemed worn out from bearing seven children in eleven years, but today it seems probable that she had some form of cancer. Alfred was sent to the Wises at Woodchester, so that she would have one less to cope with, and no doubt also because the family realised that her final illness would be extremely distressing for him. The news reached Woodchester that she had died on his twelfth birthday.

The sense of loss, of betrayal, of confusion, for the child of twelve can only have been agonising. There is nothing whatever about it in Housman's writings. But it certainly shaped his philosophy of life.

Now Edward's redoubtable cousin Lucy stepped into the breach.

Sophie Becker, his 'closest lady friend'

She decided to marry Edward Housman herself, and take Sarah's seven young children under her own wing.

It cannot have been an easy task, with Edward becoming increasingly unreliable. But she found an ally in the young Alfred. Probably Sarah had spoken to him before she died, about his responsibility as the eldest. She certainly did this with, for instance, Clemence, whom she asked to look after little Laurence. But Alfred at once took on the role of go-between for Lucy and her stepchildren, and must have greatly eased her arrival at Bromsgrove. Where poetry and the imagi-

Lucy Agnes Housman, 'my dearest Mamma'

nation were concerned, Lucy was as good as Sarah; she made it her business to introduce the Housman children to all the best in nineteenth century writing, and the evening story read aloud to the children became a regular daily event.

One day Alfred came to call us in to reading; some book had just been finished. "What is she going to read now?" we asked. "One of the nicest books that has ever been written," he answered. And that was our introduction to the delights of Cranford.

Laurence, who recalls that introduction to literature, also remembered a considerable variety of games led by Alfred. For instance the portrayal of the astronomical movement of sun, moon and earth by using himself and his brothers as rotating figures on the lawn. Alfred's fascination with astronomy was another life-long interest, which informs the greatest product of his adult scholarship, a five-volume edition of

Clemence and Kate

the works of the Roman astronomer-poet, Manilius.   But most of the
games were poetic. Kate writes:

> …in our childhood Alice in Wonderland first appeared, and Lear's
> Book of Nonsense, giving a lead, I think, to A. E. H.'s natural bent
> to write comic verses.

One such game was a kind of verbal charades, in which contestants
were set a series of nouns and had to write a poem linking them all
together. Laurence recalls one bout where the nouns to be introduced
were: novel, hat, banker, cucumber, yacht and, hardest of all, abridge-
ment. A. E. H's entry for this particular competition is a masterpiece
of nonsense verse:

> At the door of my own little hovel
>   Reading a novel I sat;
> And as I was reading this novel
>   A gnat flew away with my hat.
> As fast as a fraudulent banker,
>   Away with my hat it fled
> And calmly came to an anchor
>   In the midst of the cucumber bed.
>
> I went and purchased a yacht,
>   And traversed the garden tank,
> And gave it that insect hot
>   When I got to the other bank;
> Of its life I made an abridgement,
>   By squeezing it somewhat flat.
> And I cannot think what that midge meant
>   By flying away with my hat.

The literary games were not all poetry. There were themes for plays,
like this:

> Alfred's contribution was a domestic sketch in verse and prose enti-
> tled "A Morning with the Royal Family," the opening sentence of
> which ran, " ' Pigs on the front lawn!' cried the King. 'Lend me a

cannon, somebody?' Nobody lent him a cannon; so seizing a tea-spoon from the breakfast table, he rushed from the apartment."

And an attempt at a co-operative crime novel which reads like the scenario for a bout of Cluedo:

> Our first experiment of any length was a novel called "Veronica", in which each was to be responsible for a separate character; Alfred's was the villain, mine was the parish curate with a long beard beginning dark and ending light; and if I remember right, as soon as Alfred heard of the beard, the curate's fate was sealed; he was to die an early and violent death, strangled by the villain in the beautiful beard with which I had provided him.

After Sarah's death, Edward decided to move back to Fockbury, installing himself this time in the Clock House, a property which had been left jointly to all five children of the Reverend Thomas Housman. By doing this, he was in fact depriving the other four beneficiaries of an income which they should have gained from letting or selling the house. The move was probably illegal, and certainly of dubious morality. It was the beginning of serious financial difficulties.

For Alfred, however, it meant close proximity to "Housman's Hill", and it was from here that he made those evening rambles to gaze into the West, his nostalgia no doubt tinged with the memory of his lost mother.

Sarah died in 1871 and the marriage with Lucy was settled in 1873. Alfred meanwhile had become, at the age of eleven, a Foundation Scholar at Bromsgrove School, an achievement that was crucial to his future career as an internationally renowned Latinist.

The scholarship was fortuitous. Bromsgrove School, which then prided itself on being King Edward's Grammar School, Bromsgrove, for faintly spurious reasons, had gone through interesting changes immediately before his arrival. The Headmaster, Dr J. D. Collis, a great scholar, industrious empire-builder and snob, had fallen foul of the inspectors from the Board of Education. They had laid bare an abuse which to modern ears is shocking and even in those more class-ridden days was improper. Collis, who had been an usher at Rugby

under Thomas Arnold, was determined to make a Public School of
Bromsgrove, and had introduced numbers of private pupils from far
and near, as boarders and at a tidy fee. The Foundation of the School,
however, which had been set up two hundred years before by a
Restoration baronet, Sir Thomas Cookes, was intended to provide free
education for worthy children of the townspeople of Bromsgrove. The
inspectors had found that these little Foundationers were being taught
virtually as pauper children; they wore a highly old-fashioned Blue-
Coat style uniform, had their lessons in a shed segregated from the
private pupils, were taught only by a barely qualified writing master,
were forbidden the use of the private pupils' playing fields, and worst
of all, were forbidden to enter for the Oxford scholarships set up by
Sir Thomas Cookes.

In the scandal, Collis resigned and was replaced by a more cheerful
figure, though a scholarly one, Dr Blore. The latter's first aim, on taking over the school, was to clear up the anomaly of the Foundation
Scholarships. Scholars were now to be treated exactly like all the other
pupils, and thus would benefit from the best of the teaching and the
opportunity to sit for Oxford and Cambridge scholarships.

For the young Alfred, it was a lucky stroke; he was one of the first
scholars to be elected by Blore under this new deal. Edward Housman
would have been hard pressed, in his deteriorating financial situation,
to educate his five sons as private boarders. Blore did not remain long
at Bromsgrove. He moved on to King's, Canterbury, and was replaced
by Herbert Millington, the man who had the greatest influence on
Housman's early classical training, and who remained a lifelong friend.

A. E. H. at Bromsgrove was small for his age, and retiring. Kate
tells us that he was called "Mouse", and pushed about by bigger boys
who tried to stamp on his toes. But Bromsgrove in those days was a
very small school, even by nineteenth-century standards. Mr
Millington made a special feature of keeping his own eagle eye on
every boy. Brains and scholarship were the characteristics he sought
most. So A. E. H. did not seem to suffer long, and soon became a spe-
cially favoured pupil. In both poetry and the classics, his contributions
were exceptional. At the age of fifteen he won a prize for his poem
"The Death of Socrates" – his first published poem, which appeared

in the school magazine and the local paper. He won other prizes. There has been an intriguing little difference of opinion over his poem "Sir Walter Raleigh," which neatly illustrates the attention to detail shown by the present-day school of Housman experts:

Laurence Housman in his Memoir states that "Sir Walter Raleigh" did not win the School poetry prize. Kate Symons states that it did. The two leading biographers, Graves and Page, follow Laurence's line. But the leading archivist, Naiditch, shows that Kate's opinion may be more accurate, since it appears to be born out by the School List for Midsummer 1873. What are ordinary poetry-lovers to make of such scholarly study? We can only be grateful that A. E. Housman's reputation rests with authorities who believe in getting the details right.

Being a Foundation Scholar meant that Alfred could live at home as a day-boy, walking to school each morning across the fields. I once heard of a tradition in Bromsgrove that he took up the hobby of many Victorian schoolboys and walked with a vaulting-pole, to make it quicker to cross hedges and brooks. But I have never seen written evidence of this. When the other children went down with scarlet fever, however, he was told to stay at school as a boarder until the coast was clear. That he much preferred his home life with his stepmother Lucy is shown by this sad little letter from school in 1875:

> Yesterday I went into the churchyard, from which one can see Fockbury quite plainly, especially the window of your room. I was there from two o'clock till three. I wonder if you went into your room between those hours. One can see quite plainly the pine tree, the sycamore and the elm at the top of the field. The house looks much nearer than you would expect, and the distance between the sycamore and the beeches in the orchard seems very great, much longer than one thinks when one is in Fockbury.
>
> Give my love to Father, and to my brothers and sisters and believe me your affectionate son , Alfred.

When he was back home again, and she was away in London, his letter to her was more cheerful, more in his typical humorous vein. It is also an early reminder of the fact that he always referred to her as "Mamma".

22nd April 1875

My dear Mamma,
  I cannot say
That much, since you have gone away,
Has happened to us, so of course
I must fall back on that resource, –
That great resource, which o'er the earth
Precedence holds, and which is worth
All oher topics put together,
I mean, (I need not say) T H E W E AT H E R .

This is only the opening of a very long letter in verse. He was sixteen years old at this time. There are many recorded examples of the influence he continued to exert over the literary progress of his little brothers and sisters. Laurence especially set great store by his big brother's approval:

Voice from the corner: "Excellent!" And because of that single word of commendation, those lines, and those alone - the result, I suppose, of my reciting them to myself so may hundreds of times - have remained in my memory - Alfred having said that they were excellent.

He does not always suggest, however, that Alfred's supervisions were wholly disinterested. When Edward Housman eventually decided to move back to Perry Hall in Bromsgrove, the children each adopted their own climbing tree in the overgrown orchard of the lower garden. One day Alfred climbed up the branches of Laurence's tree:

Alfred came up into my tree and told me I was to write a sonnet. I did not know what a sonnet was; but he having one to give away (for I think that was the explanation) I was to write one, and take over by thought transference his as mine. He had a tough task, stuffing it down my throat and getting it out again...It was not, I am sure, 'love's divine self-abnegation' which made him hand over to me, hard bit by bit, that poem of is own composition to be signed as mine. He had written a poem which he did not think good enough for himself; but he did not want it to be lost.

When Edward Housman left Clock House in Fockbury, to return to central Bromsgrove, he sold the place in his own interest , and immediately engaged in further improper financial dealings. He was persuaded at an auction of Perry Hall to mortgage himself to the hilt, and turned now to the Wise family of Woodchester to help him out. The eldest son of the family, Edward Tuppen Wise, Alfred's senior by eight years, was persuaded to service this mortgage. Clock House itself was not actually sold until two years later. Only an unwise man would have taken on such a liability. The Wise family were incensed, and rightly so, because Edward Housman failed to repay the loan on the terms agreed. The disagreement led to a rift bewteen the Housmans and the Wises, and Alfred felt obliged, whatever his personal feelings, to take his own father's side. It was ten years before he was able, after his father's death, to take up the friendship again; ten years in which he sorely needed such friends as the Wises had been to him.

Meanwhile, after seven years of rigorous tutorial by Herbert Millington, the young A. E. H. was the equal of any classical student in the land. For one of his prizes at Bromsgrove he received a copy of Benjamin Kennedy's Sabrinae Corollae, which he said was an important inspiration in his decsion to become a Latinist. The texts of Benjamin Kennedy, who was at that time Headmaster of Shrewsbury School and thus a Shropshire man, continued in use for almost a century, and I and many of my my post-war generation remember the minor comedies of Kennedy's Shorter Latin Primer, with its snatches of poetry as grammatical memory-aids:

> "Of Nemo may you never say
> Neminis or Nemine".

When Housman moved to Cambridge many years later, it was to become Kennedy Professor of Latin, a pleasantly poetic touch. Millington did not suffer fools gladly, but with the able and the receptive, nothing was too much trouble. To pass first in the final year's exams of your own school may or may not be a special distinction, depending on the status of the school. Bromsgrove was indeed a small school, with only a little over one hundred pupils in the entire establishment. Herbert Millington, however, was not merely a brilliant and demanding teacher of the classics; he was also a clever judge of intellectual ability, and he chose carefully. During the twenty years of his Headship, sixty of his pupils gained scholarships at Oxford and Cambridge, and twenty of his assistant masters went on to become Headmasters of well established Public Schools; an extraordinary record. One of the twenty, of course, was Kate's husband, Edward Symons.

The Annual Report of the Oxford and Cambridge Schools Examination Board for Autumn 1877 shows clearly how good a pupil A. E. Housman was: he passed six subjects, four with distinction. In the country as a whole, there were 729 candidates that year. Of these, 178 gained some form of distinction, and only twelve gained four or more distinctions. This means not only that Bromsgrove was high in the academic league for those days, but more importantly that the young Alfred was statistically in the top 1.66% of the nation. He was awarded a Scholarship to St John's College, Oxford, to read classics in what is called the Honour School of Mods and Greats, certainly then the most prestigious academic course at any European university.

Of Alfred's boyhood, Laurence recalls this general comment:

> Years after I remember Alfred saying, as we talked over the days of our childhood, "Was there ever such an interesting family as we were?" There were probably many; but none, I dare say, more interested in itself, when it stood compact and pugnaciously united - seven against the rest of the world.

And of his schooldays, this:

> Many years later I asked Alfred, who was the shining light of his sixth form, what he thought of our late Head as a teacher. "Excellent," he said,"for those of good ability in the subjects he cared about." Over the rest there was silence.

Herbert Millington had a different comment to make about A. E. Housman. On his final school report he wrote:

> May all my boys be like him.

CHAPTER TWO

ᑎᑎᑎᑎ

What passes for Latin
at Oxford

A. E. H. arrived at Oxford in 1877 conscious that he was a member of the intellectual élite. From the beginning, his work and his interests show the ironic and critical self-confidence that is still typical of the really able student today. That is not to say that he was idle; he worked extremely hard and successfully at matters which interested him. But he believed he knew his own strengths and could set his own standards. Lucy wrote from Bromsgrove to ask him to describe the Matriculation ceremony at the start of his first term. This was his reply:

> …we one by one inscribed our names in a large book, in this wise. "Alfredus Edvardus Housman, e Coll.Di.Joh. Bapt. Gen. Fil. natu max." which is, being interpreted, "A. E. Housman, of the college of St John the Baptist, eldest son of a gentleman." Sons of clergyman write "Cler.Fil." and sons of officers write "arm.fil." Then I wrote my name in English in a smaller and less dignified book, and then paid £2.10s.0d. to a man at the table, and then we sat down one by one in a row till all had written their names and paid their fee. Then an attendant brought in twenty-two copies of the Statutes of the University, bound in violet, and piled them on the table hiding the Vice-Chancellor from the eye. Presently his head appeared over the top, and we got up and stood in a sort of semicircle in front of him. Then he called up each of us by name and presented each with a copy of the Statutes, and with a paper on which was written in Latin, or what passes for Latin at Oxford:-"At Oxford, in the Michaelmas Term A.D.1877, on the 13th day of the month of October: on which day Alfred Edward Housman of the

Alfred as a young man

College of St John the Baptist, gentleman's son, appeared in my presence and was admonished to keep the laws of this University…
…As to keeping the statutes contained in the violet cover, you may judge what a farce that is when I tell you that you are forbidden to wear any coat save a black one, or to use fire-arms, or to trundle a hoop, among other things.

Already he knew what good Latin was, and knew that his mentors often did not. He attended a lecture by the great Benjamin Jowett, Master of Balliol, who had inspired this famous little satire:

"My name is Jowett
And this is my college,
What I do not know
Isn't knowledge."

But A. E. H. was incensed by Jowett's careless grammar and apparent ignorance of the niceties.

Nor did he have any intention of sticking to his own academic subject. He tried his hand at poetry, but with mixed success. Under the pen-name of "Tristram" he wrote humorous verse and prose for an undergraduate magazine called Ye Round Table, and in another called Waifs and Strays he produced two of his better poems, "Parta Quies", which we shall meet again, and "New Year's Eve". In 1879 he entered for the Newdigate Prize, the most celebrated Oxford undergraduate poetry competition. His entry, "Iona", came third.

Another letter to Lucy before the end of his first term describes with relish one of John Ruskin's celebrated art lectures - nothing to do with Latin nor Greek, but magnificent entertainment:

This afternoon Ruskin gave us a great outburst against modern times. He had got a picture of Turner's, framed and glassed, representing Leicester and the Abbey in the distance at sunset, over a river. He read out the account of Wolsey's death out of Henry VIII. Then he pointed to the picture as representing Leicester when Turner had drawn it. Then he said, 'You, if you like, may go to Leicester to see what it is like now. I never shall. But I can make a pretty good guess.' Then he caught up a paintbrush. 'These stepping stones of course have been done away with, and are replaced by a be-au-ti-ful iron bridge.' Then he dashed in the iron bridge on the glass of the picture. 'The colour of the stream is supplied on one side by the indigo factory.' Forthwith one side of the stream became indigo. 'On the other side by the soap factory.' Soap dashed in. 'They mix in the middle-like curds,' he said, working them together with a sort of malicious deliberation. 'This field, over which you see the sun setting behind the abbey, is now occupied in a P R O P E R manner.' Then there went in a flame of scarlet across the picture, which developed itself into windows and roofs and red brick, and

Moses Jackson

rushed up into a chimney. 'The atmosphere is supplied – thus!' A puff and cloud of smoke all over Turner's sky, and then the brush thrown down, and Ruskin confronting modern civilisation amidst a tempest of applause…

Doubtless neither Lucy nor Edward Housman had much idea of what was going on at Oxford; but Edward, who was always short of cash, would not have disapproved of the following postscript to one of Alfred's letters to him:

P.S. The Union authorities decline to supply one with stamps up to more than a certain weight. Such is my wiliness that I intend to frustrate their parsimony by posting this letter in T W O envelopes, differently directed. I have numbered the sheets of this letter, that you may not be confused.

Alfred was in the Union often, and has recorded a number of hot political debates, there and on the hustings, which he clearly enjoyed watching. But it was not politics that brought about his downfall. At first all went very well. In 1879 he took Honour Moderations, got his First Class, and embarked on the second two years of the Oxford classics course, Literae Humaniores, or Greats. A word of explanation may be necessary:

Classics at Oxford was uniquely a four-year rather than three-year course. The first two years, or Honour Moderations, is a linguistic course where the candidate studies the Latin and Greek written languages, concentrating on syntax, grammatical forms, imagery, and all those exact nuances of language that have made the classics a by-word for the teaching of precise thought. At this, A. E. H. excelled. The second half of the course consists of the study of classical philosophers and political thinkers, and is based upon the analysis of literary thought. Housman disliked this. All his life he said that he was a textual critic, and tried to avoid the analysis of literature as such. What made him a great classical scholar was his ability to interpret and correct the words on the page, not his ability to clarify the opinions and imaginings of poets and thinkers.

It was in the second part of this course that A. E. H. began deliberately to transfer his interests to other things.

Of the small number of good friends he made at St John's, two need special mention. Arthur Pollard was, like Housman, a classicist and became in later life Keeper of Printed Books at the British Museum as well as a life-long correspondent. The other, Moses Jackson, was also a scholar of the college, but in science not classics. He was in appearance everything that Housman was not; tall, fair-haired, with boyish good looks, and an outstanding athlete. These three friends shared digs together in their more senior Oxford years, and at some time during this period A. E. H. began to understand that he had fallen in love with Moses Jackson. One of the most beautiful poems in A Shropshire Lad uses the Ancient Greek myth of Echo and Narcissus to portray the love that A. E. H. felt:

Look not in my eyes, for fear
 They mirror true the sight I see.
And there you find your face too clear
 And love it and be lost like me.
One the long nights through must lie
 Spent in star-defeated sighs,
But why should you as well as I
 Perish? gaze not in my eyes.

A Grecian lad, as I hear tell,
 One that many loved in vain,
Looked into a forest well
 And never looked away again.
There, when the turf in springtime flowers,
 With downward eye and gazes sad,
Stands amid the glancing showers
 A jonquil, not a Grecian lad.

Homosexuality in 1880 was a serious matter; it was illegal, and shortly
after this time Housman would be alarmed by the trial and imprison-
ment of Oscar Wilde, for declaring publicly a feeling for Lord Alfred
Douglas that was close to his own for Moses Jackson. Modern journalistic accounts of Gay Rights have confused the issue, as far as
Housman is concerned. There is an assumption that homosexuals
must either be wildly promiscuous, or else suffering from deep-seated
psychological disturbance, or a mixture of both. With Housman, one
quickly learns that his nature was so complex and so private that any
sweeping conclusion about his love-life is almost certain to be wrong.
Other biographers have looked at this from a variety of angles, but
there is one aspect of Housman's make-up which, it seems to me, they
all overlook. It is this:

 When Shakespeare wrote,

   Let me not to the marriage of true minds
   Admit impediment... ,

he hit upon a feature of high scholarship that modern students of sex
ignore; a person of great intellectual powers, coupled with great cultural sensitivity, needs someone of like mind on whom to fasten his

affection. Or, put another way, when a brilliantly clever person meets an equally clever friend who is "on the same wavelength", he often begins, for that very reason, to find such a person attractive. Whether the brilliantly clever friend is male or female is a matter of chance. But today it is comparatively easy to find a friend of the opposite sex who is equally well-educated and "on the same wave-length". In Housman's day, it was nearly impossible. One of the greatest arguments, I have always believed, for the equal education of the sexes is that it enables young people to build a marriage upon genuine community of interests, not upon material things such as the need to produce a family or get one's dinner cooked. Housman's predicament neatly illustrates this problem. Moses was not only extremely good-looking; he was also a scholar of the college and a well-informed conversationalist.

But one also gains a strong impression, in Housman's emotional life thus far, that the people with whom he had a close relationship, fulfilling both his need to love and his need to share the enthusiasms of his intellect, were mostly women; his mother, Lucy, Kate, Sophie Becker, the Wise girls. Later in life he met, here and there, women who became close friends - in spite of his often caustic remarks about womenkind in general - but who were kindly and homespun like his sister-in-law or Jeannie, or socialites, like Alice Rothenstein.

At Oxford, however, when he most needed to share the emotional experience of his very real powers, there were no women in evidence. Even if there had been, they would not have been able to talk knowingly to him.

I do not say that this is the whole reason for Housman's homosexuality; far from it. But in a world of boarding Public Schools, complete segregation into adulthood, officers' messes, gentlemen's clubs and student common rooms where women were spoken of as a different form of animal life, it goes some way to explain why so many intellectuals of those days were secret homosexuals.

In Last Poems, which came out in 1922, A. E. H. himself dared to publish the following verse, which expresses his view on the public indecency laws. I quote only the first half of it:

St John's College, Oxford

The laws of God, the laws of man,
　　He may keep that will and can;
Not I: let God and man decree
　　Laws for themselves and not for me;
And if my ways are not as theirs
　　Let them mind their own affairs.
Their deeds I judge and much condemn,
　　Yet when did I make laws for them?
Please yourselves, say I, and they
　　Need only look the other way.
But no, they will not; they must still
　　Wrest their neighbour to their will,
And make me dance as they desire
　　With jail and gallows and hell-fire.

Now, ever since Housman's homosexuality became public knowledge, there has been an assumption that this was the reason for his failure in the Oxford final exams. But it seems doubtful. Probably the new feelings of love were a distraction, especially since, as it turned out, Moses Jackson himself was far from being homosexual. But in 1881 they were still on the friendliest of terms. There were other upsets, such as the news, shortly before the exams that his father had had a stroke.

But Arthur Pollard, who knew better than anyone what was going on, put it down to lack of work on the syllabus and over-confidence. For night after night, while Arthur was busy revising, Alfred and Moses were chatting. Moses had already completed his three-year course in physics, with First Class Honours, and had nothing to lose. Only Alfred was building up trouble. Captivated by the charm of Moses, he was wasting his time.

Disliking the set books, A. E. H. now turned to something that interested him more; the study of the Latin author Propertius. It took a lot of his time and was certainly painstaking and original work, but entirely outside the syllabus. This is not an unusual happening at Oxford, where long before and long since there have been instances of able students who became diverted on to researches more to their own liking than the set works.

Whatever the combination of reasons, when the final exams came,

Bromsgrove School

A. E. H. was hopelessly unprepared, had to leave out whole questions, and was failed outright.

It was the second great disaster of his life. Years later he himself wrote, "They had no option but to plough me."

He returned to Bromsgrove in disgrace, without a degree and with no visible source of income. Herbert Millington, who knew his real strength, took pity on him and gave him a part-time job teaching the Sixth Form. His family, who had anticipated a triumphant return and a substantial future salary to help with their financial troubles, must have been bitterly disappointed, though they do not seem to have shown it publicly.

Now A. E. H. set about redeeming himself. He became withdrawn and morose, the silent recluse whom so many met in after years. But he settled down and took the Oxford pass degree in a year, and then sat the competitive exam for entry to the Civil Service. This too he passed and was offered an appointment as a Higher Division Clerk, first in Dublin, which he refused, and then in the Patent Office in London, which he accepted for a very cogent reason: Moses Jackson was now employed there.

It was a job of a kind, and it brought continuing friendship. But it would have been better if he had not been so high-handed over "what passes for Latin at Oxford."

CHAPTER THREE

ↀↀↀↀ

In London Streets the Shropshire name

MOSES JACKSON had taken lodgings in Bayswater with his younger brother Adalbert. In 1882, A. E. H. moved in with them. For a decade, he now lived quietly in London and spent his office hours badgering away as a Patent Office Clerk. It sounds boring, and biographers of Housman have tended to represent this part of his life as sterile and unrewarding, a penance for his shortcomings at Oxford. This could be a misrepresentation. The Patent Office was staffed with able graduates - such as Moses with his First Class Honours in physics, and who was now Examiner for Electrical Specification. I know two former Patent Office officials, and they are among the most cultured, imaginative and amusing friends that I possess.

To a man of such exceptional intellectual powers as Housman, however, it could have been less than challenging. None of his letters relate what went on at the Patent Office, but at least one from a friend, which we shall see, suggests that he enjoyed good company there. But the academic career which he sought now seemed remote, and the environs of Bayswater must have seemed barren indeed to a man whose romantic instincts lay in the lovely rolling country West of Severn. The poems that he came to write only a few years later are full of references to the loneliness of London. In A Shropshire Lad Number XXXVII for instance:

> You and I must keep from shame
> In London streets the Shropshire name;
> On banks of Thames they must not say
> Severn breeds worse men than they;
> And friends abroad must bear in mind
> Friends at home they leave behind.

And again in Number XLI:

> Yonder, lightening other loads,
> The seasons range the country roads,
> But here in London streets I ken
> No such helpmates, only men;

And in Number L:

> By bridges that Thames runs under
> In London, the town built ill,
> 'Tis sure small matter for wonder
> If sorrow is with one still.

And Number LI:

> We neither knew, when we were young,
> These Londoners we live among.

But there were compensations. He had the company of Moses, and of Adalbert too, for A. E. H. developed a close friendship with the younger brother.

The life also left sufficient time for study. In the evenings A. E. H. would go up to the British Museum library in order to continue his own textual researches in the Latin authors that most interested him. These studies were the crucial factor in his subsequent rise to scholastic eminence. In 1883 he published the first, Horatiana, analyses of the Roman writer Horace.

This lifestyle ran smoothly until 1885. In June that year he wrote a particularly cheerful letter to Lucy, which shows all the irony and wit of his Oxford days, combined with the gory interest in death that pervades so much of his later poetry:

My dear Mamma,
You would never guess what I was doing on Tuesday week: serving on a Coroner's Jury. This comes of having one's name on the register of voters. Civil Servants I believe are exempt from serving on ordinary Juries, but not Coroner's. Of course for once in a way it is

rather amusing, and it is not likely to happen oftener than about once in four years. We sat on five bodies: one laundryman who tied a hundred-weight sack to his neck and tipped over into the water-butt; one butcher's man who cut his throat with a rusty knife and died a week after of erisepylas (moral: use a clean knife on these occasions); one old lady who dropped down in a fit; one baby who died in convulsions; and one young woman who died of heart dis-ease after eating onions for supper. I really do not know what is the good of a jury or of witnesses either: the Coroner does it all: his mind seemingly is lighted by wisdom from on high, so he tells the Jury what their verdict is and the witnesses what their evidence is: if they make mistakes he corrects them. The butcher's man had a brother-in-law: he looked radiantly happy: a member of his family had distinguished himself, and he was revelling in the reflected glory.

But that autumn there happened an odd and unexplained incident which seems to have been a turning point. For a week, Housman van-ished. Nobody today knows where he went or what he did. Did he stay in London and walk the streets? Did he find an unknown Patent Office friend to put him up on a sofa? Or did he sleep rough at night under bridges?

More important, why did he vanish? Everybody seems to agree that he had had a tiff with the Jacksons, and walked out. The more circum-spect biographers have suggested that it could just have been an ordi-nary domestic quarrel. But Moses Jackson was alarmed, since he took the unprecedented step of writing to Alfred's sick father to try to dis-cover his friend's whereabouts.

The significant fact is that when he resurfaced, A. E. H. had decid-ed to leave the Jacksons. Within a week he had moved out, and took lodgings briefly in Northumberland Place, and then in Highgate with a landlady named Mrs Hunter, at Byron Cottage, 17 North Road. The first great love poem of A Shropshire Lad, written before the rest took shape, dates from this year. It was "Bredon Hill", set in South Worcestershire but later included with the Shropshire poems because it chimes in so well with the nostalgic and lovelorn themes of the oth-ers. We shall meet it in a later chapter. It is filled with the irony of

Laurence Housman as a young man

chances missed and happiness that has fled away - like this little poem
from ASL:

> With rue my heart is laden
>   For golden friends I had,
> For many a rose-lipt maiden
>   And many a lightfoot lad.
>
> By brooks too broad for leaping
>   The lightfoot boys are laid;
> The rose-lipt girls are sleeping
>   In fields where roses fade.

It is hard not to speculate about this incident. The circumstances seem
to hint that Alfred had come to the point of making some kind of a
declaration of love to Moses, and that the latter had told him this was

not reciprocated and could not go on. We can only guess at the truth. Two years later Moses Jackson left the Patent Office in order to take up an apppointment as Principal of the Sind College in Karachi, then part of British India. It was the parting of the ways.

> Oh, when I was in love with you,
>   Then I was clean and brave,
> And miles around the wonder grew
>   How well I did behave.
> And now the fancy passes by,
>   And nothing will remain,
> And miles around they'll say that I
>   Am quite myself again.

A Shropshire Lad Number XVII suggests the end of a transient affair. But perhaps Number XII from More Poems came nearer to the truth:

> I promise nothing: friends will part;
>   All things may end, for all began;
> And truth and singleness of heart
>   Are mortal even as is man.
>
> But this unlucky love should last
>   When answered passions thin to air;
> Eternal fate so deep has cast
>   Its sure foundation of despair.

In 1889, Moses returned to England briefly to get married, but he and Adalbert resolved not to tell A. E. H. about it. Poor Alfred only learnt the news by letter after Moses and his new wife had returned to Karachi. But A. E. H. continued to correspond with Moses until the latter's death thirty-four years later, in 1923, so he certainly forgave him.

A happier event was the reconciliation with the Wise family, and visits to Woodchester had a cheerful and stabilising influence on Alfred's otherwise inward-looking mind:

My dear Mrs Wise,
Here I am (or as our lively neighbour the Gaul would say, me voilà

arrivé.) I had a very good journey (bon voyage), as the weather
improved and I found a through carriage to London (Londres) so
that there was no need to change at Swindon
(Swindres), after which the train stopped nowhere, not even at
Reading (Lisant)..... .

One wonders whether, in the absence of Moses, Sophie Becker did not
become the object of some tenderness, in spite of being fourteen years
older - somewhere between a girlfriend and an elder sister. To write
her a poem in German, he must have been fond as well as clever:

> ...I enclose a cloak room ticket for Miss Becker and also a poem
> which I have written in her own beautiful language: please tell her
> this, because otherwise she may not know it: I assure her that it is a
> fact. Give my love to all, or at least to all to whom it may with pro-
> priety be given, and believe me yours affectionately,
> A. E. Housman

Now he plunged himself back into textual research, and a series of
articles appeared in learned Classical journals - a series so impressive
that by 1892 he had made his name something to be reckoned with, if
not in London streets, then at least in the Classics faculties of the universities. When his chance came to get back into the academic life, no
less than seventeen classical specialists, some of them the leading pro-
fessors of Latin and Greek, were happy to give him a reference.

❧❧❧❧

CHAPTER FOUR

I have the honour to present myself

IN 1892 the Professor of Latin and Greek at University College, London, died. The University decided to separate the two chairs, and advertised Professorships in Latin and Greek separately. This was A. E. Housman's application:

> 19 Apr 1892 To the Council of University College, London

My Lords and Gentlemen,

I have the honour to present myself as a candidate for the vacant Professorship of Latin in University College. If however the Latin chair should be conferred on another I would ask to be considered as an applicant in that event for the Professorship of Greek. I am thirty-three years of age. I entered the University of Oxford as a scholar of St John's College in 1877; in 1879 I was placed in the first class in the Honour School of Classical Moderations; in 1881 I failed to obtain honours in the Final School of Literae Humaniores. I have since passed the examinations required for the degree of B.A. and am of standing to take the degree of M.A. in the event of my appointment to a Professorship. In 1881 and 1882 I was for some time engaged in teaching the sixth form at Bromsgrove School, and in the latter year I obtained by open competition a Higher Division Clerkship in Her Majesty's Patent Office, which I now hold. During the last ten years the study of the Classics has been the chief occupation of my leisure, and I have contributed to the learned journals many papers on ancient literature and critical science.....

He then named twelve groups of learned articles, both Latin and

University College, London, one hundred years ago

Greek, which he had published during the last five years in journals of national and international standing. The application was supported by seventeen testimonials, including those of Professor Nettleship of Oxford and Professor Mayor of Cambridge, and ending with his good friends Arthur Pollard, with whom he had studied, and Herbert Millington, who had been his Headmaster, his employer and his rescuer.

Most of the testimonials came from people who did not know him personally, but admired his research. One keeps coming back to this astonishing fact; the work he had been doing in the evenings, after business hours, for his private satisfaction, was of such value that it took him from Patent Office Clerk to Professor at a major University in one single leap.

After Housman died there was found among his papers a treasured letter of this time. It was from a simple, trusted friend in the Patent Office, John Maycock. A. E. H. had clearly been deeply touched by it:

It is funny to think how I used to chaff you about your work producing no money, and all the time you were working silently on, with that strength of purpose which I can admire but can't imitate...As a rule English people never allow themselves to say or write what they think about anyone, no matter how much of a pal he may be. Well, I am going to let myself loose. I like you better than any man I ever knew. There is, as   far as I could discover, absolutely no flaw in your character as a man. I don't say this only on my own account, but I can see how you can stick to a friend like you have to Jackson.

Now Housman had achieved what he truly wanted – the life of a senior university academic. He threw himself enthusiastically into the activities of the College. In 1895 and 1897 he was Dean of the Faculty of Arts and Law. He lectured by invitation to the Literary Society, on such subjects as Matthew Arnold, the Spasmodics, Erasmus, Darwin, Robbie Burns, Tennyson, and Swinburne; all rather surprising since he regarded himself as a textual not a literary critic.

One of the first responsibilities of a newly-appointed professor was to deliver his Introductory Lecture. He gave it the title, "Reasons for Acquiring Knowledge." The lecture was given before the Faculties of Arts, Law and Science, was a great success, and was printed by the College in the same year. The conclusions he came to in the lecture were, broadly, that knowledge was an end in itself, and acquiring it was good for Man. In an age when men of substance believed that it was more important to have a trained mind than to be an expert in anything – that "an able man was an able man whatever his discipline," - this conclusion struck a chord with popular academic opinion.

As a teacher, however, he already showed that preoccupation with his subject, and lack of interest in his students, for which he later became notorious. He could not remember their names, and explained that to him the difference between the second and fourth declensions was more important. He wrote laughingly to Mrs Rothenstein, the wife of his friend the painter William Rothenstein, that he had noticed that his Jewish students were particular about staying away from College to keep their religious holidays - especially those on which the Derby and the Oaks were taking place.

For Housman, research and publication were infinitely more important than teaching. He now began the long series of major publications that made his academic reputation: studies on Propertius in 1893, which concluded the work he had begun as an undergraduate at St John's; an edition of Juvenal in 1905; and in 1903 the first volume of his edition of the Astronomica of Manilius.

Since this latter work was his greatest work of scholarship, it requires a little explanation. Manilius was a quirky choice. It is somehow typical of Housman that he should have decided to devote a lifetime of study to a peculiar late-Roman poet, whose life's work was an attempt to interpret in mathematical terms the workings of the stars, and to set the whole thing in verse. Housman had always had a knowledgeable interest in astronomy, as we saw in his boyhood. But he himself was sometimes contemptuous of Manilius' errors of judgement and stilted expression. Enoch Powell, who was both a student of Housman and briefly a colleague, has portrayed Housman as being so vibrantly sensitive to the poetry of Horace, Propertius, Catullus or Virgil that he could scarcely master his emotions sufficiently to read them aloud to his students. Yet he chose for the main impetus of his research a far lesser poet in Manilius.

Behind all this there still lay hidden to the public gaze the humorist and wit, as Kate Symons described retrospectively:

> A. E. H. possessed a great faculty for seeing the humorous side of things; and from his boyhood onwards he was prone to write frivolous rhymes and nonsensical skits on passing topics. These careless absurdities, written without pains, come into peculiar contrast with the sombre tone of his published poetry, and the polished accuracy of his scholarly writings. But it can do no wrong to the scholar and the poet to show that he had within him a fund of comedy to temper the more apparent severities that he imposed upon himself.

Having heard that Laurence, now a published poet in his own right, had written some Devotional Poems, A. E. H. wrote delightedly to Lucy that he was having a go himself, for the Salvation Army. Here are two of his versions:

> There is Hallelujah Hannah
>   Walking backwards down the lane,
> And I hear the loud Hosanna
>   Of regenerated Jane;
> And Lieutenant Isabella
>   In the centre of them comes,
> Dealing blows with her umbrella
>   On the trumpets and the drums.

And this one:

> 'Hallelujah!' was the only observation
> That escaped Lieutenant-Colonel Mary Jane,
> When she tumbled off the platform in the station,
> And was cut in little pieces by the train.
>> Mary Jane the train is through yer:
>> Hallelujah, Hallelujah!
> We will gather up the fragments that remain.

However much he enjoyed the scholastic life, from this time on he nevertheless preserved a private and quiet world where human company would not disturb his inward pain, his nostalgia for happiness past - those "happy highways where I went, And cannot come again."

Byron Cottage became, as it were, a secret lair where none should come to shatter his daydreams.

There were a number of sad losses and disasters during his eighteen years at University College. In 1892 Adalbert Jackson died of typhoid. He was only twenty-seven. A. E. H. had become almost as friendly with Adalbert as he had with Moses, and the former shared his elder brother's blonde good looks and athleticism. Some have even speculated as to whether A. E. H. did not transfer to Adalbert his physical affection. In recollection, A. E. H. wrote a poem entitled "A. J. J.", published as Number XLII in More Poems, of which these are the last two verses:

> Strange, strange to think his blood is cold
>> And mine flows easy on,
> And that straight look, that heart of gold,
>> That grace, that manhood gone.

> The word unsaid will stay unsaid
>> Though there was much to say;
> Last month was time enough: he's dead,
>> The news must keep for aye.

In 1894 Edward Housman died, alcoholic and financially broke. Now A. E. H. had to think of Lucy and his brothers and sisters, making himself responsible for their finances when possible.

Then in 1895 there came the trial of Oscar Wilde. A. E. H. must have felt the deepest bitterness about its relevance to his own situation. But it must certainly also have had the effect of convincing him that his private life should remain truly private. Even at his death forty years later, it seems unlikely that his surviving sisters had any idea of his sexual orientation, and only Laurence could have guessed.

Laurence published in Additional Poems, after Alfred's death, this remarkable poem by his elder brother, with shades of Wilde's "Ballad of Reading Gaol" and Kipling's "Danny Deever". If you substitute for "the colour of his hair" some such phrase as "the nature of his love", you can see how strongly Housman felt about the cruelty of the persecution of homosexuals:

Oh who is that young sinner with the handcuffs on his wrists ?
And what has he been after that they groan and shake their fists?
And wherefore is he wearing such a conscience stricken air?
Oh they're taking him to prison for the colour of his hair.

'Tis a shame to human nature, such a head of hair as his;
In the good old time 'twas hanging for the colour that it is;
Though hanging isn't bad enough and flaying would be fair
For the nameless and abominable colour of his hair.

Oh a deal of pains he's taken and a pretty price he's paid
To hide his poll or dye it of a mentionable shade;
But they've pulled the beggar's hat off for the world to see and stare,
And they're haling him to justice for the colour of his hair.

Now 'tis oakum for his fingers and the treadmill for his feet
And the quarry-gang on Portland in the cold and in the heat,
And between his spells of labour in the time he has to spare
He can curse the God that made him for the colour of his hair.

The Boer War produced another grievous blow; A. E. H.'s youngest brother Herbert, now a sergeant in the King's Royal Rifles, was killed in 1901. His death inspired the most moving of all Housman's war poems, "Illic Jacet" - in English "Here Lieth…" – which he had cause to use again in the Great War, as we shall find. The following poem, "Astronomy", with its strange interplay between the Southern Cross in the sky and the cross one has to bear, was also inspired by Herbert's death:

> The Wain upon the northern steep
>   Descends and lifts away.
> Oh I will sit me down and weep
>   For bones in Africa.
>
> For pay and medals, name and rank,
>   Things that he has not found,
> He hove the Cross to heaven and sank
>   The pole-star underground.
>
> And now he does not even see
>   Signs of the nadir roll
> At night over the ground where he
>   Is buried with the pole.

Four years later Robert died. He, too, was young, only forty-four. He had been on an expedition from Bath to Iford Manor, a beauty spot in a deep combe, where a lovely brook runs beneath a graceful arched bridge.

He had climbed down into the brook to take a photograph of the manor, had slipped, fallen in the water, and caught a chill from which he died. His death seems ignominious compared to Herbert's, but shocking nonetheless.

Then in 1907 Lucy died, "My dearest Mamma." She was eighty-four, so her end cannot have been entirely unexpected. But the Housman children owed more to her than to anyone, and it must have saddened Alfred greatly. She had inspired a voluminous correspondence from him, and surely lent him the trust and self-belief to keep going in the face of adversity.

Through all this, the compensations were considerable. Apart from the reputation he was now making as a scholar of national standing, he had lively company, had discovered an interest in gourmet wining and dining, was entranced by his first voyage abroad, to Paris, Rome and Naples in 1897, and last but not least, had become quite unexpectedly a popular, published poet.

ɛ/ɔɛ/ɔɛ/ɔ

The winds out of the west land blow

A MAN so private as A. E. Housman was unlikely to make public confessions about his poetic inspiration. He denied, in a famous letter in 1933 to Maurice Pollet, that A Shropshire Lad sprang from a sense of emotional loss. To suggest instead that it all came from passing physical sensations like "a relaxed sore throat" was his way of protecting his privacy:

> I have never had such a thing as a crisis of pessimism. In the first place, I am not a pessimist but a pejorist (as George Eliot said she was not an optimist but a meliorist); and that is owing to my observation of the world, not to personal circumstances. Secondly, I did not begin to write poetry in earnest until the really emotional part of my life was over; and my poetry, so far as I could make out, sprang chiefly from physical conditions, such as a relaxed sore throat during my most prolific period, the first five months of 1895.

But in that spring of 1895, three years into his first Professorship, with Moses Jackson eight years in India, and Byron Cottage as a clandestine Aladdin's cave of dreams, Housman experienced a sudden upsurge of the creative spirit, such as happens only to a few great poets. The poems poured forth one after another.

What came welling up into his mind was the view to the distant West from his Worcestershire childhood home. There in his memory he wandered, the prospect of a Promised Land seeming to be brought in on the wind:

Byron Cottage,Highgate

The winds out of the west land blow,
　　My friends have breathed them there;
Warm with the blood of lads I know
　　Comes East the sighing air;

- the opening verse of Number XXXVIII.

That he did also walk a great deal is now certain, though he only seldom describes his walks. Kate Symons draws attention to the romance in his country rambling; the purpose of his path was to find a beautiful view:

> One evening in a summer of glorious sunsets, when he was staying at the Lansdown Grove Hotel, he came into 20 Belmont to say we must go to Lansdown with him to see the after-glow break over Bath. Off we went up the hill as the sun was setting, and arrived in the fields leading to Beckford's monument in time to witness a soft, rosy after-glow suffuse the towers and spires of Bath – a lovely sight that otherwise I should never have seen, making Bath appear like the city of a vision.

In June 1897 he was in Bromsgrove for the Queen's Diamond Jubilee – exactly ten years after the scene he describes in the first poem of A Shropshire Lad. And this is his account to Lucy:

> On the evening of the 22nd I started at eight in the evening for Clent, and got to the top of Walton Hill about 9.20. The sky was fairly clear, and so was the air to the North, but hazy Southwards: Malvern had been invisible all day. (On Saturday when the rain was about I saw as good a view from Walton Hill as I ever saw, the Sugar Loaf and Black Mountain and Radnor Forest quite plain.) One or two private bonfires started before the time, but most of them waited for 10 o'clock. Five minutes or so after the hour I easily counted 67.

After his death, Laurence described A. E. H. in old age:

> …his walking powers, which all his life had given him that quiet companionship of nature which suited him best, had considerably diminished…

But in February and March of 1895, alone in Byron Cottage after a day at University College, and with only the circumspect Mrs Hunter discreetly in the background, it was in his memory that A. E. H. relived those walks. No poem in A Shropshire Lad expresses this better than "Far in a Western Brookland," my own favourite:

Far in a western brookland
    That bred me long ago
The poplars stand and tremble
    By pools I used to know.

There in the windless night-time,
    The wanderer, marvelling why,
Halts on the bridge to hearken
    How soft the poplars sigh.

He hears: no more remembered
    In fields where I was known,
Here I lie down in London
    And turn to rest alone.

There by the starlit fences,
    The wanderer halts and hears
My soul that lingers sighing
    About the glimmering weirs.

Behind his boyhood home at Perry Hall there lay an extensive brookland, an area of marshy water-meadow fed by the Spadesbourne Brook
and the Battle Brook, uniting in a series of pools beneath the willows.
It is easy to imagine the scenes that were passing through Housman's
mind as he wrote.

His first plan had been to link the poems by suggesting an imagi-
nary narrator, who was to be called Terence Hearsay. Two of the
poems mention Terence as a speaker or being spoken to. It was Arthur
Pollard – loyal and wise friend from Oxford days – who told him that
the proposed title, "Poems of Terence Hearsay", was a bad idea. He
suggested instead "A Shropshire Lad", a suggestion that must have
been an important contribution to the book's success. Arthur also
advised A. E. H. to try his own publisher, Kegan Paul, since his first
approach to Macmillan had proved fruitless.

A year later, in March 1896, Housman published A Shropshire Lad,
at his own expense, but under Kegan Paul's imprint. Within two years
it was sold out, and for the second edition A. E. H. was approached by

an irrepressibly bumptious young publisher called Grant Richards, who was trying to make a name for himself by taking up the latest poets - including Thomas Hardy.

Richards had that kind of young man's infectious enthusiasm, coupled with a refusal to be downcast by the poet's rudeness, which Housman found endearing. Thereafter, he used Grant Richards as his publisher through thick and thin. He scolded him often, in round terms, for his mistakes in printing, for his inconsistencies over copyright, and for his attempts to introduce editions that would be greater moneyspinners. For Housman was resolute in insisting that he did not want to make money out of his poems, and that he did want them to be available in cheap editions for young people.

But he also found in Richards a splendid travelling-companion, who shared his own interests in French "haute cuisine", in good wine, in beautiful Mediterranean towns. He paid Richards the highly unusual compliment of joining his family, boisterous young children and all, on holiday in Cornwall. And when Grant Richards teetered on the verge of bankruptcy, he used his own money to bail him out.

The success of A Shropshire Lad caused Housman to think that he ought to check up on some of the geographical details, and several walks ensued, to places mentioned but not hitherto visited. Hughley Church and its non-existent steeple, near Much Wenlock, was the worst case; he wrote to Laurence late in 1896:

> I ascertained by looking down from Wenlock Edge that Hughley Church could not have steeple. But as I had already composed the poem and could not invent another name that sounded so nice, I could only deplore that the church at Hughley should follow the bad example of the church at Brou, which persists in standing on a plain when Matthew Arnold has said that it stands among mountains. I thought of putting a note to say that Hughley was only a name, but then I thought that would merely disturb the reader. I did not apprehend that the faithful would be making pilgrimages to these holy places.

It really did surprise him that anyone should make a pilgrimage to places of his invention. Forty years later he was still explaining away the anomalies, to a wildly enthusiastic young American, Houston Martin, for instance:

> I am Worcestershire by birth: Shropshire was our western horizon, which made me feel romantic about it. I do not know the county well, except in parts, and some of my topographical details are wrong and imaginary. The Wrekin is wooded, and Wenlock Edge along the western side, but the Clees and most of the other hills are grass or heather. In the southern half of the county, to which I have confined myself, the hills are generally long ridges running from north to south, with valleys, broad or narrow, between.

And to Maurice Pollet, the more painstaking French "professeur de lycée", who would have appreciated the great Classical scholar's reference to Tyrtaeus, the Athenian historian of Sparta:

> I know Ludlow and Wenlock, but my topographical details – Hughley, Abdon under Clee - are sometimes quite wrong. Remember that Tyrtaeus was not a Spartan.

It was to Maurice Pollet that Housman described the literary sources whose influence he admitted:

> No doubt I have been unconsciously influenced by the Greeks and Latins, but I was surprised when critics spoke of my poetry as 'classical'. Its chief sources of which I am conscious are Shakespeare's songs, the Scottish Border Ballads and Heine.

But in the same letter comes the denial that the poems are autobiographical:

> The Shropshire Lad is an imaginary figure, with something of my temper and view of life. Very little in the book is biographical.

Some enthusiasts for Housman see his wanderings as something like those of Thomas Hardy - whom he much admired - in the sense that his landscapes appeared to be wild moorland, heath and upland pasture. A recent newspaper feature in the Times was illustrated by a photograph of the Long Mynd, which Housman does not mention and which is very like Hardy country but quite unlike Housman country. Housman's hills are not like Hardy's. They are viewpoints from which a more pastoral and agricultural landscape can be studied, and Housman's walks are among windy woods and hedgerows. "Loveliest of trees..." is most typical of this:

> Loveliest of trees, the cherry now
>   Is hung with bloom along the bough,
> And stands about the woodland ride
>   Wearing white for Eastertide.
>
> Now of my threescore years and ten,
>   Twenty will not come again,
> And take from seventy springs a score,
>   It only leaves me fifty more.
>
> And since to look at things in bloom
>   Fifty springs are little room,
> About the woodland I will go
>   To see the cherry hung with snow.

"On Wenlock Edge...", the poem that most inspired Vaughan Williams, has all the Shropshire themes in one; woodland gales, distant views, a hint of classical archaeology, the glories that are past, the troubles that remain for the wandering narrator:

> On Wenlock Edge the wood's in trouble;
>   His forest fleece the Wrekin heaves;
> The gale, it plies the saplings double,
>   And thick on Severn snow the leaves.
>
> 'Twould blow like this through holt and hanger
>   When Uricon the city stood:
> 'Tis the old wind in the old anger,
>   But then it threshed another wood.
>
> Then, 'twas before my time, the Roman
>   At yonder heaving hill would stare:
> The blood that warms an English yeoman,
>   The thoughts that hurt him, they were there.

There, like the wind through woods in riot,
  Through him the gale of life blew high;
The tree of man was never quiet:
  Then 'twas the Roman, now 'tis I.

The gale it plies the saplings double,
  It blows so hard, 'twill soon be gone:
Today the Roman and his trouble
  Are ashes under Uricon.

The new popular interest A. E. H. accepted with impish glee. It was not, after all, his serious life work, but a spare time enthusiasm. The poems themselves no doubt represented deep feelings needing urgent expression. But once they were out, he could afford to be more detached. His family were delighted. To Laurence, whose first volume of poetry, Green Arras, had been published before A Shropshire Lad, he wrote smugly about his complimentary reviews:

> …There is rather a good notice in last week's Sketch. I thought the New Age review very nice, except the first paragraph disparaging the other chaps.

The American poet Witter Bynner wrote with great enthusiasm to enquire whether Mr Housman was to publish any more poems, and whether his profession had had an influence on the verse of A Shropshire Lad. A. E. H.'s reply is revealing:

My Dear Sir,

You seem to admire my poems even more than I admire them myself, which is very noble of you, but will most likely be difficult to keep up for any great length of time… As to your inquiries: I wrote the book when I was thirty-five, and I expect to write another when I am seventy, by which time your enthusiasm will have had time to cool. My trade is that of professor of Latin in this college: I suppose that my classical training has been of some use to me in furnishing good models, and making me fastidious, and telling me what to leave out. My chief object in publishing the verses was to

give pleasure to a few young men here and there, and I am glad if
they have given pleasure to you.

There now began a series of small confusions – cases of mistaken iden-
tity – between Alfred and Laurence. A. E. H. found them irritating
and amusing at one and the same time. His letter to Laurence in
December of 1896 sums it up, and ends with an ironic barb:

> …Last night at dinner I was sitting next to Rendall, Principal of
> University College Liverpool and Professor of Greek there, a very
> nice fellow and a great student of Marcus Aurelius and modern
> poetry. He was interested to hear that you were my
> brother: he said that he had got Green Arras, and then he proceed-
> ed, "I think it is the best volume by him that I have seen: The
> Shropshire Lad had a pretty cover."
> I remain
>   Your affectionate brother (what a thing is fraternal affec-
> tion, that it will stand these tests!)   A. E. Housman
>
> P.S. After all, it was I who designed that pretty cover; and he did
> not say that the cover of Green Arras was pretty. (NOR IS IT.)
>
> P.P.S. I was just licking the envelope, when I thought of the follow-
> ing venomed dart: I had far, far rather that people should attribute
> my verses to you than yours to me.

But Housman's new-found fame as a poet also brought him a wider
and far more interesting circle of friends, a fact which he owed in some
part to Laurence's reputation, as well as his own. They included
Thomas Hardy, Robert Bridges, Edmund Gosse and Wilfrid Scawen
Blunt, and also the portraitist and Royal Academician William
Rothenstein. He never liked the portrait Rothenstein did of him, and
this was the cause of a slight cooling in friendship later, although he
continued to correspond in friendly fashion with Mrs Rothenstein. He
wrote warmly to congratulate her – her, not him – when Rothenstein
was knighted. But by and large these were all deeply creative people,

whom Housman admired and liked, and who had a broadening influence on his thinking.

His sister Kate, however, disliked the gloomy sentiments in A Shropshire Lad, a fact which made him laugh:

> Kate writes to say that she likes the verse better than the sentiments. The sentiments, she then goes on to say, appear to be taken from the Book of Ecclesiastes. To prefer my versification to the sentiments of the Holy Ghost is decidedly flattering, but strikes me as a trifle impious.

But he did not know of her other comment, to Laurence. Concerned by Alfred's aloofness and morbidity ever since his Oxford failure, she wrote delightedly, on reading A Shropshire Lad :

> "Alfred has a heart!"

CHAPTER SIX

છ૭છ૭છ૭

A name on the lips of men

J.E.B. MAYOR, the Professor of Latin at Cambridge who had been one of Housman's referees eighteen years earlier for the University College post, died in 1910. Housman was nominated for his Chair. This time, there was no need for referees and applications. He was already "a name on the lips of men", and was elected without further ado both to the Professorship and to a Fellowship at Trinity College. For the remainder of his life-the next quarter of a century-Trinity, Cambridge, was his home. Within a few months of his election, the Chair of Latin was renamed the Kennedy Professorship, in honour of Benjamin Kennedy whose Sabrinae Corollae had been so formative an influence in Housman's schooldays.

For twenty-five years Housman became increasingly famous, increasingly admired, and to some increasingly notorious. But the fact that he did not again move his centre of work, and that life in the courts of a Cambridge college is to many people narrow and introspective, does no justice to the infinite variety of his personality. Apart from Housman the far-famed scholar, there was Housman the cantankerous, Housman the traveller and gourmet, Housman the compassionate, Housman the self-critically modest, and Housman the atheist, who nevertheless maintained the tenderest respect for things of the spirit. To each of these contrasting Housmans I have devoted a separate chapter. This one is concerned with the far-famed scholar.

The phrase "a name on the lips of men" was Housman's own. It comes from a rare example of his formal prose. In 1919 he was invited by the Fellows of Trinity to write the tribute to his colleague Henry Jackson, on the latter's retirement. In some respects, it could have been his own tribute:

A. E. H. in 1911

...In Trinity, in Cambridge, in the whole academic world and far beyond it, you have earned a name on the lips of men and a place in their hearts to which few or none in the present or past can make pretension. And this eminence you owe not only or chiefly to the fame of your learning and the influence of your teaching, nor even to that abounding and proverbial hospitality which for many a long year has made your rooms the hearthstone of a Society and a guesthouse in Cambridge for pilgrims from the ends of the earth, but to the broad and true humanity of your nature, endearing you to old and young, responsive to all varieties of character or pursuit, and remote from nothing that concerns mankind...

The highlights of his tenure of the Chair of Latin were, for a layman such as myself, the following: the Inaugural Lecture of 1911, the explanatory lecture "The Application of Thought to Textual Criticism" of 1921, the edition of the works of Lucan in 1926, the completion of his exhaustive study of Manilius in 1930, with the publication of the fifth and last volume, and the surprising and controversial lecture, "The Name and Nature of Poetry" in 1933.

There were, of course, a vast number of lesser publications. "Praefanda" was an analysis of obscene words used by classical Roman poets, and was due to be published by the Classical Quarterly magazine. But they had cold feet when they saw its contents, and the study was only published some time later by a German periodical. It is a unique example of Housman allowing his private, hedonistic instincts to peer out through the protective screen of his pure scholastic research.

The Inaugural Lecture, like the Introductory Lecture at University College in 1892, was a sort of compulsory statement of policy on the part of a new professor. Years later the lecture was published under the title, "The Confines of Criticism", which explains to the layman pretty much what it was about. The title was not Housman's own; he felt unable to publish it in his own lifetime, even though it had been very well received, because there was in it a single reference to Shelley's poetry, which he remembered but could not find in writing. It is an instance of his own scholarly rigour and precision. It hinged upon the word "summer", included in later editions of Shelley's poems but omitted in a version Housman owned. It seems a small reason for not allowing such an important statement to be published:

> ...it contains a statement which I cannot verify. Not far from the beginning of this century I saw, in some literary journal I suppose, an account of an autograph, or some early impression, of Shelley's 'O world, O life, O time,' in which the eighth line ran 'Fresh spring and autumn, summer and winter hoar'; and this I now cannot trace.

The message of the Inaugural Lecture may be summed up: Textual criticism is a science, not a branch of literature.

It was the principle lying behind all his work, and which emerges in "the Application of Thought to Textual Criticism" as well. When he crossed this divide himself, he often made mistakes. For instance, the following piece of advice he gave to Grant Richards:

> I have not finished Proust's book, but I have read enough to form the opinion that an English translation would not sell, and, apart from that, could not be really satisfactory, as the merit of the French is in great part a matter of diction and vocabulary.

It was an error of literary judgement. Proust's "A la Recherche du Temps Perdu", and particularly "Du côté de chez Swann" translated as "Swann's Way", was as a result turned down by Richards and passed to another publisher, for whom it became a best-seller. Richards lost a good deal of money by taking Housman's advice.

There are other moments when A. E. H. was after all able to recognise his limitations, like this letter to Seymour Adelmann in which he withdrew from an attempt to give a pronounced literary judgement:

> I can no more define poetry than a terrier can define a rat; but he knows a rat when he comes across one, and I recognise poetry by definite physical sensations, either down the spine, or at the back of the throat, or in the pit of the stomach.

Of this emotional definition-this poetry-in-the-guts-there was to be one great, final outburst. Towards the end of his life, in 1933, he was persuaded against his better judgement to accept an invitation to give the Leslie Stephens Memorial Lecture at Cambridge. This was an annual literary event, held in Housman's case in the Senate House, to which men of letters could be expected to flock from far and wide. One can only speculate as to why Housman agreed to do this. It was against his stated principles, something for which he had always felt ill-equipped. It caused him great heart-searching, and not a little trouble in the preparation.

Perhaps he felt, as an old man, that he had nothing to lose. His life's work was over, he had only routine lecturing to occupy him; so many friends and correspondents had lauded his poems to the skies, in opposition to his own modest instincts; and perhaps also he was irritated by the school of literary criticism just then coming to the fore in Cambridge, and wanted to fire off a counterblast.

The new approach to the study of literature put forward by two young English dons, F. R. Leavis and I. A. Richards, was to become in the thirties and after the Second World War a major movement in English teaching everywhere. It was based upon a more analytical and structured breakdown of the art of writing, and by no means approved the idea that poetry could be recognised only by "physical sensations, either down the back of the spine, or at the back of the throat, or in the pit of the stomach."

Housman called his lecture "The Name and Nature of Poetry". He stated that poetry was not the thing said, but a way of saying it. Poetry was not the same as verse, and simile and metaphor were inessential to it. The lecture persistently shied away from any precise statement as to what exactly a poem was; "poems are poems". As to the creation of a poem, he said that this was "in its first stage... less an active than a passive and involuntary process..."

And again "...a secretion; whether a natural secretion like turpentine in the fir, or a morbid secretion, like the pearl in the oyster." In his own case, he made it plain that his poetic creativity was morbid like the pearl in the oyster. In an earlier letter comes this: "I have seldom written poetry unless I was rather out of health, and the experience, though pleasurable, was generally agitating and exhausting." It was not calculated to please Leavis and Richards, who were said to have remarked, on leaving the Senate House after the lecture, that their work had been set back by ten years.

Housman's own version of this appears in a letter to Laurence:

> The leader of our doctrinaire teachers of youth is reported to say that it will take more than twelve years to undo the harm I have done in an hour.

This Romantic and anti-intellectual view of poetry seems quite untypical of Housman the scholar. It represents the most important instance of his own complexity and variety, especially since his knowledge of poetry of every kind was voluminous, as in this event recalled by Laurence:

His memory of poetry was as extraordinary as his memory of architecture. One day we were discussing Keble, a poet for whom naturally he had no great liking...I happened to have mentioned the
hymn which begins 'Sun of My Soul', saying that it only formed
part of a whole poem, the first verse of which I was unable to
remember. Immediately he quoted it with unhesitating correctness.

Furthermore there had been, during his last years at University
College and the earlier years at Trinity, a good deal of secret poetry of
his own–morbid secretions, one might say. In 1920 word came from
British Columbia, where Moses Jackson had emigrated after India, in
order to run a farm. Moses was ill with cancer. Once again there was a
period of "continuous excitement". Poems came surging forth.

The Boer War had produced a flurry of poetry, especially with the
death of Herbert, but after that there had been only a trickle. By 1922,
however, A. E. H. had enough poems, of a standard good enough in his
opinion for publication, to produce a second volume, to be sent to
Moses. It was to be called Last Poems, presumably because he wanted
to make it plain to his readership that they could expect no more after
this. The considerable number of good poems that remained were in
fact published after his death by Laurence, under the titles More
Poems and Additional Poems.

Grant Richards produced a first edition of Last Poems of four thousand copies. Even by modern standards, this is a large edition, and
Housman thought it much too large. But by the end of the year it had
run into several more editions and 21,000 had been sold. A. E. H. was
extravagantly hailed as England's Greatest Poet. Yet in the same year
T. S. Eliot published The Waste Land, a poem to make Housman seem
decades out of date. In spite of this, Housman reviewed The Waste
Land very favourably.

The opening poem of Last Poems was entitled "The West", and
took up the theme of the tender but painful world towards the setting
sun, at the point where A Shropshire Lad had left it. Only this time,
one cannot help but feel that there is a place a good deal further West
than the Clee Hills; Canada, where Moses was dying. These are the
last two verses:

Wide is the world, to rest or roam,
　　And early 'tis for turning home:
Plant your heel on earth and stand,
　　And let's forget our native land.

When you and I are spilt on air
　　Long we shall be strangers there;
Friends of flesh and bone are best:
　　Comrade, look not on the West.

In 1923 Moses died. He had inspired a host of passionate and tender verse. "Epithalamium", Number XXIV in Last Poems, containing the following lines within a longer poem, had been written twenty-five years earlier on the news of Moses' marriage:

Home return who him behold,
　　Child to mother, sheep to fold,
Bird to nest from wandering wide:
　　Happy bridegroom, seek your bride.

By way of contrast, the last great volume of Manilius was to contain a dedication to Moses consisting of twenty-eight lines of Latin elegiac verse. Tragically, it would have meant nothing at all to Moses, who never seems to have been a lover of poetry and certainly could not read the classics. Just as sadly, it meant nothing to Moses' Canadian descendants, who to this day appear to resent the connection between Housman and their ancestor. Although Moses' own moral behaviour towards Alfred seems to have been irreproachable, and although he inspired some of the most moving short poems in the English language, they have preferred to keep Housman enthusiasts at arms length.

As for poor Housman, after the death of Moses he left this:

He would not stay for me, and who can wonder?
He would not stay for me to stand and gaze.
I shook his hand and tore my heart in sunder
And went with half my life about my ways.

 භ භ භ

Like an absconding cashier

AFTER Moses Jackson's death, even more than before it, Housman's public manner was one of gloomy reticence, morbidity and rudeness. The greatest number of acquaintances and chance encounters were those who knew him least, and therefore saw only his prickly side. Such a one was Max Beerbohm, socialite, wit, critic and author of saucy and satirical works such as Zuleika Dobson. Not surprisingly, he found he had nothing in common at all with Housman the cantankerous, and wrote this:

> He was like an absconding cashier. We certainly wished he would abscond – sitting silent and then saying only "there is a bit of a nip in the air, don't you think?"

The story spread far and wide that Professor Housman was a boor. Those who knew him well understood better, but they were few in number. One such was Wilfrid Blunt. Laurence had been relaying to Alfred some detail of his supposed rudeness, and tells this story:

> It was probably when I told Alfred what he had done that I quoted Wilfrid Scawen Blunt's comment on him in his reminiscences: Alfred struck him as one who did not wish to open his mouth unless obliged. "That," said Alfred, "is absolutely true." And considering how often, in spite of that wish, he did open his mouth and make himself quite pleasant to comparative strangers, he ought to be regarded, if not as one of the most genial, at least as one of the most self-sacrificing of men…

Blunt also wrote to a mutual friend, S. C. Cockerell:

We all liked Housman when he was here a week ago, though anything less like a Shropshire Lad would be impossible to conceive.

The man who bore the brunt of Housman's withering complaints was Grant Richards. He probably made sufficient money from being Housman's publisher to feel that it was worth shouldering all the grumbles. Even so, he seems to have been remarkably good-humoured and thick-skinned. Here is an early example, and of course the "nefarious publisher" mentioned in it was Richards himself:

> My dear Richards,
> Pray who gave Mr E.Thomas leave to print two of my inspired lays in his and your Pocket Book of Poems and Songs? I didn't, though he thanks me in the preface. Just the same thing happened in the case of Lucas' Open Road, issued by the same nefarious publisher. You must not treat my immortal works as quarries to be used at will by the various hacks whom you may employ to compile anthologies. It is a matter which affects my moral reputation…

It has to be said that Housman could himself be quite inconsistent, which made it hard for Richards. His attitude towards the great throng of composers who wrote to ask for permission to set his poems to music, and to present them in various forms of their own conception, well illustrates this. Sometimes his response was obliging but cynical:

> Mr Balfour Gardiner may publish 'The Recruit' with music if he wants to. I always give my consent to all composers, in the hope of becoming immortal somehow.

And sometimes it was surprisingly accommodating, for instance when he allowed Vaughan Williams to print his text in full although it was normally contrary to his strict policy:

> As to Mr Vaughan Williams, about whom your secretary wrote: he came to see me, and made representations and entreaties, so that I said he might print the verses he wanted on his programmes. I mention this lest his action should come to your ears and cause you to set the police after him.

But he changed his tune when he saw what Vaughan Williams had done:

> …I am told that composers in some cases have mutilated my poems, - that Vaughan Williams cut two verses out of "Is my team plough-ing". (I wonder how he would like me to cut two bars out of his music), and that a lady whose name I forget has set one verse of "The New Mistress", omitting the others. So I am afraid I must ask you, when giving consent to composers, to exact the con-dition that these pranks are not to be played.

A. E. H. hated the idea that composers should regard their settings as somehow more important than the poems themselves, just as he hated any kind of swank and self-importance. Poor Ivor Gurney, the most modest of poets and composers, was organist at Gloucester Cathedral, and made the mistake of writing for permission on the cathedral head-ed notepaper. This was Housman's response:

> My dear Richards,
> Mr I. B. Gurney (who resides in Gloucester Cathedral along with St Peter and Almighty God) must not print the words of my poems in full on concert programmes (a course which I am sure his fellow-lodgers would disapprove of); but he is welcome to set them to music, and to have them sung, and to print their titles on pro-grammes when they are sung.

He was strict with the B. B. C. in refusing permission for his poems to be read, but ironically resigned if they were to be sung:

> I don't allow the wireless people to recite my poems, but as I allow the poems to be sung to music there is no reason why the songs should not be broadcast. I daresay the music is spoilt, but that is the composer's look out; and the words are mostly inaudible.

Another breed of artist about whom Housman was caustic was those who made a living from illustrating books. Richards had allowed a popular edition of A Shropshire Lad to be distributed with illustra-tions by an artist, Lovat Fraser, who had seen to fit to dress the charac-ters in brocade silks and powdered wigs:

…The trouble with book-illustrators, as with composers who set poems to music, is not merely that they are completely wrapped up in their own art and their precious selves, and regard the author merely as a peg to hang things on, but that they seem to have less than the ordinary human allowance of sense and feeling. To transpose into the 18th century a book which begins with Queen Victoria's jubilee is the act of a rhinoceros.

And to Seymour Adelmann he summed it all up:

Neither illustrators nor composers care twopence about words, and generally do not understand them.

A more gleeful but nevertheless biting attack on an illustrator came with the publication of a new book by his friend Frances Cornford, authoress of, "Oh, fat white woman whom nobody loves, Why do you walk through the fields in gloves…". The book was entitled Death and the Princess, and the frontispiece portrayed the princess assailed by a vast, horned and cloven-footed woodland god representing Death. It amused Housman to interpret these two characters rather differently:

…I suppose you have seen Mrs Cornford's new book. Her portrait in the frontispiece is pleasing and recognisable, but Cornford's is almost a caricature…

Frances Cornford was one example amongst many of women friends whose intellect he both admired and mocked. His view of women's rights was greatly coloured by the behaviour of his sister Clemence. She was a leading activist in the Women's Suffrage Movement, and whatever A. E. H. thought about the ethics of the case, his prim and reticent nature loathed the public antics that the suffragettes got up to. Laurence, who aided and abetted Clemence in all this, wrote of A. E. H.'s opinion of women:

What my brother Alfred describes as the deplorable sex.

Another woman friend, Lily Thicknesse, sent A. E. H. a copy of a book named The Rights and Wrongs of Women. It released from his pen a flood of cynicism:

Dear Mrs Thicknesse,   ...

My blood boils. This is not due to the recent commencement of summer, but to the Wrongs of Women, with which I have been making myself acquainted. 'She cannot serve on any Jury'; and yet she bravely lives on. 'She cannot serve in the army or navy' – oh cruel, cruel! – 'except' – this adds insult to injury – 'as a nurse.' They do not even employ a Running Woman instead of a Running Man for practising marksmanship. I have been making marginal additions. 'She cannot be ordained a Priest or Deacon': add 'nor become a Freemason'. 'She cannot be a member of the Royal Society': add 'nor of the Amateur Boxing Association'. In short your unhappy sex seem to have nothing to look forward to, except contracting a valid marriage as soon as they are 12 years old; and that must soon pall.

When Laurence tried his luck at getting A. E. H. to lend the weight of his name to the suffrage movement by signing an appeal, the latter refused with these words:

> ...Even if I were actually in favour of women's suffrage in the abstract I think I should like to see some other and less precious country try it first: America for instance, where the solution ought to be just as urgent as here.

It hardly seems like the man who had treasured a warm relationship with his mother and Lucy, with Kate and the Wise sisters, with Sophie Becker and Mrs Hunter. Even in his later years at Cambridge he made close and surprising friendships with young women – for instance the seventeen-year-old Joan Thomson, daughter of the Nobel Prize Winner and physicist J. J. Thomson. But then, these were highly intelligent women to whom he could talk on his own terms. Nor were all his women friends of the Cambridge years particularly well-educated. Basil's wife Jeannie was homely rather than cerebral, but Alfred felt more at home in her household than in any other. Percy Withers and his wife, late friends with whom he stayed often at this time, also provided a haven of relaxation. When Mrs Hunter, his landlady at Byron Cottage, moved to Pinner, he moved with her in spite of the increased travelling time from University College.

There is a curious incident of Housman's University College days which reveals much about his supposed misogynism. He was chairing a meeting of the college debating society, at which the motion for debate was that women should be enfranchised. The society's records show that the house was equally divided when it came to the vote, but that the motion was in the end carried. The explanation can only be that the chairman used his casting vote to support the motion.

Another facet of Housman's reputation for dullness surely arose from his public utterances. His routine lectures were said to be excruciatingly boring, though Enoch Powell would deny this. The Leslie Stephen Lecture caused him weeks of anxiety. Yet it is also on record that when the mood took him, amongst friends, he could be the wittiest of speakers. When Basil asked him to be his best man, on the occasion of his wedding to Jeannie, Laurence had this to report:

> He greatly disliked having to make speeches, though he made them well. I think I only heard him once, when he spoke as best man, at my brother Basil's wedding, and commended the custom of a certain African tribe, which he said made a religious practice of eating the mother-in-law at the wedding feast. It was a good instance of his humour, which always had 'a bite' in it. One of the mothers-in-law was present, the other was absent; he was on friendly terms with both.

On another famous occasion he actually decided to speak where no speech was called for. There are many versions of this story, but this is Laurence's own:

> ...at a dinner where speeches were not expected but where the wine had been good, Alfred rose slowly to his feet and, to the amazement of all, began speaking. And this, I am told, is what he said: "There were two things it was very difficult to meet in Cambridge a hundred and twenty years ago; the one was Wordsworth drunk, the other was Porson sober. I am a better scholar than Wordsworth; I am a better poet than Porson. Here I stand halfway between Wordsworth and Porson." He sat down again; it was a short speech, but it was a great success.

Social gatherings were a nightmare for Housman. He dined mostly with the Fellows at High Table in Trinity, but this sometimes necessitated sitting next to a guest who did not know him. On a notorious occasion, some poor Junior Fellow or College Steward placed him next to Sir James Barrie, author of Peter Pan, thinking no doubt that the two crotchety old men of letters might have something in common. The result was a stony silence throughout the meal. The next day Housman received a note from Sir James brought by a College messenger. This is Grant Richards' version of the correspondence:

Dear Professor Houseman
I am sorry about last night, when I sat next to you and did not say a word. You must have thought I was a very rude man; I am really a very shy man
Sincerely yours,   J.M.Barrie.

The messenger returned with the following reply:

Dear Sir James Barrie,
I am sorry about last night, when I sat next to you and did not say a word. You must have thought I was a very rude man; I am really a very shy man.
Sincerely yours,   A.E.Housman

P.S. - And now you've made it worse for you have spelt my name wrong.

Another notorious brush with a scholar of international repute occurred when, so legend has it, the philosopher Wittgenstein was taken ill with a stomach upset. Because his rooms were on the same landing as Professor Housman, and because the nearest lavatory for general use was several floors downstairs, he sent his bedmaker - or room servant - to ask for permission to use the Professor's private lavatory on the same floor. Housman recoiled in horror from the idea of sharing his lavatory with anyone, and refused. Poor Wittgenstein was left to deal with his little problem as best he could.

The worst kind of social gathering for Housman was the mixed house-party. He obliged his close friends when he had to, but decided

Clemence and Laurence Housman, in 1951

on one occasion to put his foot down with Mrs Rothenstein. His refusal of her invitation must be one of the rudest on record:

Dear Mrs Rothenstein,
People are asking me out a great deal too often, and you are one of the chief offenders. I am not a social butterfly like you: nature meant me for solitude and meditation (which frequently takes the form of going to sleep): talking to human beings, whether 'lovely ladies' or not, for any length of time leaves me in a state of prostration, and will finally undermine my health unless I take care. By declining your invitation for next Wednesday I calculate that I shall make you very indignant, and then you will leave me severely alone for a long time, which may save me from premature decease…

We can presume that Alice Rothenstein knew her man, however, and was too big-hearted to be offended for long.

From time to time scholars and students of English wrote to ask for permission to write Housman's biography, or more modestly to do a little research on his poetry. This too offended his sense of decency and privacy, and he persistently refused. Grant Richards was instructed to disclose nothing at all to such people:

> Tell him that the wish to include a glimpse of my personality in a literary article is low, unworthy and American. Tell him that some men are more interesting than their books but that my book is more interesting than its man. Telrude and Wilfrid Blunt found me dull. Tell him anything else that you think will put him off.

If the request came from an American University, for all of which Housman had a deep-seated Old-World contempt, the refusal was caustic:

> I strictly enjoin you to tell Miss Shirley Pratt nothing. The sham education given at American Universities has resulted in my receiving about half-a-dozen similar enquiries from its victims.

His family, of course, were not exempt from his ironies, especially when Laurence was engaged on one of his Christian themes. The latter wrote for students at University College a series of religious plays, the Little Plays of St Francis, which had a good deal of success, both in the College and at the Glastonbury Festival. Laurence took part in them himself, and was to play the leading role in the final scene of St Francis' death:

> I sent word of it to Alfred at Cambridge, and asked him to come and see me perform. He replied that, though my death had attraction for him, he could not face the journey to London in the cold of winter, or tear himself from the College Feasts which were taking place at that season.

Alfred's loss of faith and consequent cynicism about death, resurrection and the After Life was undoubtedly a part of the morbidity and contrariness from which he suffered. The poem "God's Acre", another of those which he refused to publish in his lifetime, brings out all the sadness of this intellectual standpoint:

Morning up the eastern stair
Marches, azuring the air,
And the foot of twilight still
Is stolen toward the western sill.
Blithe the maids go milking, blithe
Men in hayfields stone the scythe;
All the land's alive around

High Table at Trinity College Hall

Except the churchyard's idle ground.
There's empty acres west and east,
But aye 'tis God's that bears the least:
This hopeless garden that they sow
With the seeds that never grow.

Why, then, did Housman so dislike any society apart from the narrow one he had chosen for himself? The answer lies certainly in the disappointments and tragedies of his earlier life, but also in a not uncommon attitude amongst people of great mental powers: he had so much resource and interest within his own mind that he did not need to have others around him. He found lightweight company distracting and upsetting to his natural creativity. It is a notion somewhat alien to the British, who have never really understood intellectuals, and regard them as unsporting creatures. In France or Germany, Housman's aloofness would have been respected as normal and necessary in a great thinker, and he would probably have been able to avoid rudeness in order to obtain the isolation that he needed. A few of Housman's associates did understand this, and to them he was trusting and grateful. Laurence tells a story that well summarises the outlook of Housman the "absconding cashier":

I was staying a couple of nights with a friend in Cambridge; on the second day I said I was going round to see my brother. He looked at me amazed. "I thought you were not on speaking terms," he said. I asked why, and this was his explanation: One day my friend, meeting Alfred for the first time, having been placed beside him at high table in Hall at Trinity, made the mistake of introducing himself with the remark, "I have the pleasure of knowing your brother, Mr Laurence Housman." To which Alfred stiffly replied, "Knowing my brother Laurence is no introduction to ME." I laughed. It was so characteristic of him. "It only meant," I said, "that the poor man didn't want to have the trouble of talking to you; or else, possibly, that he disliked you at first sight, and chose that as the most direct way of avoiding conversation."

ↄﻌↄﻌↄﻌↄ

Malt does more than Milton can

WHEN Housman left University College London, a group of his former students presented him with a silver cup on which was inscribed,

> Malt does more than Milton can
> To justify God's ways to man.

The quotation is from the last-but-one poem of A Shropshire Lad, and in choosing it those students had surely recognised a merry side to their often lugubrious professor; he was also a gourmet and epicure of some reputation. The wining-dining-travelling adventurer in Housman comes as a great surprise. Yet he wrote on several different occasions, to a variety of people over a number of years, about what he regarded as his pleasure-loving self. For instance, to J. B. Priestley in 1924:

> …I wish people would not call me a Stoic. I am a Cyrenaic; and for the Stoics, except as systematisers of knowledge in succession to the Peripatetics, I have a great dislike and contempt.

A Cyrenaic is to all intents and purposes what most of us call an Epicurean – one who lives for the here-and-now, and takes a sophisticated view of whatever pleasures are immediately available. This is especially true of good food and wine. A. E. H. became a real authority on French gastronomy, and was especially partial to sea food, which explains why Frederic, the manager of the Tour d'Argent restaurant in Paris, named a dish after him. "Barbue Housman" consists of brill cooked in a cheese and white wine sauce.

Most, but not all, of A. E. H.'s letters on the subject of food are to

Grant Richards, with whom he shared this interest. They often met in France to dine together and compare notes, and if the letters sound rather like the gazetteer notes of a cookery writer, that was because Richards did indeed publish guides to touring and eating in France. This letter on Venice is from 1910:

> In Venice I almost always go to the Europa, which has absolutely the best possible situation and is not too large. In dignity, according to my gondolier, it ranks next to Danieli's, where the food and drink are better, but which is noisy, and not central enough, and dearer. A cheaper hotel, which I hear well spoken of, is the Luna, close to the royal palace; I have been inside it and it struck me as well managed. The best restaurant, to my thinking, is the Vapore, and my gondolier tells me that all foreigners say the same. From the piazza you go under the clock and along the Merceria till you come to a high bridge over a canal; there instead of crossing it, you turn sharp to the left. Much greater simplicity is to be had at either of the two Giorgiones, one near San Silvestro and one near the Santi Apostoli; but the food is not very appetising, except the Baccala pizzicato (salt cod mashed up with milk and pepper) which they have on Fridays.

And this from 1914, just before the War began, describes a tour on the western Mediterranean coast of France. The Gourmet's Guide, for which he takes Richards to task, was one of the latter's own books:

> …I ate much bouillabaisse, the best at Isnard's, the next best in the suburb of L'Estaque; but in several places it was not so good as at Foyot's in Paris. Brandade I did not think much of, and Aioli at Pascal's was rather nasty, perhaps because lukewarm. The Gourmet's Guide on Marseilles is full of blunders…

A few days later he was fulminating about gross inaccuracies in yet another guide:

> …The really outrageous thing is the fairy-tale on p. 104 about a wine called Pouilly Suisse after the proprietor of a vineyard, both non-existent. The wine is Pouilly-Fuissé…

La Tour d'Argent Restaurant, the home of Barbue Housman

But it was Paris and central France that he knew best of all, and the next letter from 1929 is typical:

> The best meal was at the Gastronome at Clermont-Ferrand. In Paris I was not best pleased with the Belle Aurore, where they made me ill, perhaps with the very poor caviar: when I ordered fraises des bois, of which they had run short, they offered me a mixture of raspberries with what they had left, thinking apparently that I should know not the difference. But the place is thoroughly and pleasantly French, and the hors d'oeuvres look as if one could lunch entirely on them. The Grand Veneur is good though its plats regionaux are not an exciting selection. At the place in Place St Michel I was disgusted with a pretended Sole Normande smothered with mushrooms, of all things in the world, and tasting exactly like the usual sole de la maison of a Parisian restaurant. The best cook-

ing that I found was at the Escargot. Avoid Clos Vougeot 1915: for
some reason it has turned out badly, as did Lafite 1900.

Back at Trinity, he was an exacting critic of the fare on High Table,
but attended College Feasts with great relish. In 1919 he joined the
exclusive Cambridge dining club, "The Family", which had only
twelve carefully chosen members, and he continued to attend their
dinners until his death in 1936. He was especially fond of oysters:

> I will remember you at midnight, when I shall be drinking to absent
> friends in stout and oysters, which are very salubrious, and which I
> take medicinally to neutralise the excesses of Christmas. When you
> give Mrs Winslow's soothing syrup to a baby, 'the little darling
> wakes up as bright as a button'; and so do I on New Year's Day.

This was from a letter to Percy Withers refusing his invitation to
spend New Year, and cheerfully explaining that after Christmas he
needed to recover from his habitual over-indulgence. "Mrs Winslow's
baby syrup" was widely advertised at that time for babies with windy
tummies. In 1934, elderly and with little in life to look forward to, he
wrote to Kate Symons:

> I am looking forward to my usual Christmas gluttony. Which
> reminds me of a great calamity. For years it had been my chief
> ambition to be invited to the Colchester oyster-feast: this year I was
> invited, but had a lecture which prevented me from going.

A few weeks later, and just after Christmas, he wrote to Percy Withers
bemoaning his inability to enjoy his food and drink. It is amazing to
discover that at the age of seventy-five, he was still taking a cold bath.

> On your expert advice I left off alcohol for a week, with no effect
> except the production of gouty symptoms, or symptoms which I
> am accustomed to regard as such. Your other recipe, a cold douche
> after my warm bath, is impracticable, because my bath is cold.

Housman's expertise as a gourmet necessitated, of course, an equal
expertise as a traveller. He was never a traveller, it should be said, in
the sense that the term was used in the British Empire. He never lived
and worked abroad, never visited Asia, Africa or the New World, never

explored unknown regions. He was strictly a tourist, in the eighteenth century sense, when educated gentlemen undertook the Grand Tour for their education. Housman's travel was restricted to the great cultural centres of civilised Europe – though he did once take the Orient Express as far as Constantinople.

But he learnt to know thoroughly well, and with the eye of a scholar, those places he did visit. His first tour, in 1897, was to Paris, Rome and Naples. He enjoyed it so much that thereafter he travelled in Europe every year. His first visit to Venice, in 1900, was a revelation. He went again each year until 1908. As usual, he took great delight in criticising the pretentious and admiring the simple and genuine; in the following letter to Lucy during that first visit, he is attacking Venetian Gothic architecture:

> Of this the Doge's Palace is the great example; you know its stupid general design, like a clothes horse with a blanket on it; I am bound to say that the reality is better than the pictures, because one can see that the flat and tame upper half of it is composed of red and white marble, although the pattern is no better than you see on the cottages in the Stourbridge Road at Bromsgrove.

And in 1926, after a quarter of a century, he wrote to Kate his last letter from Venice:

> I was surprised to find what pleasure it gave me to be in Venice again. It was like coming home, when sounds and smells which one had forgotten stole upon one's senses; and certainly there is no place like it in the world: everything there is better in reality than in memory. I first saw it on a romantic evening after sunset in 1900, and I left it on a sunshiny morning, and I shall not go there again.

A. E. H.'s knowledge of architecture was as voluminous as his knowledge of French cuisine – perhaps as his knowledge of lyric poetry. In the last year of his life he travelled, with Laurence to look after him, round some of his favourite haunts in southern France:

> We visited more places, churches, abbeys and cathedrals, than I can count. He knew them nearly all, and had a marvellous memory for

their main points of interest, and their style of architecture – even for those which he had not seen for a score of years.

The travels provided one or two curious occasions for speculation about Housman's homosexuality. Firstly, there was the gondolier Andrea, in Venice. Because A. E. H. chose to employ the same young man on each of his visits, some analysts have suggested that there was a degree of intimacy beyond the mere need to have a dependable waterman on the canals. In the letter to Lucy on his first visit, A. E. H. describes Andrea:

> My gondolier expressed a wish that he were your son. He wanted me to come to Venice next Christmas, and I explained that at Christmas I went to see you; and then he made this remark. The reason is, that if he were your son he would be well off and would have no family to provide for: so at least he says. At present he has to earn a living for one wife, two sisters, one mother, one mother-in-law, and half an uncle (who was once a champion oarsman and is now paralysed); which is pretty good for a young man of twenty-three who has had one eye kicked out by a horse.

The evidence for a homosexual relationship is scant, however. A one-eyed married man, half his age and with a large dependent family, does not seem a very likely object for a secret and illegal liaison. The notion of a "Death in Venice" scenario seems to me hopefully and romantically journalistic, but not very likely. Housman also tended to stick to the same chauffeurs for the cars he hired to tour France, but that does not imply that he had further liaisons up his sleeve. There is, however, the odd discovery of a piece of paper in his jacket pocket bearing apparently a checklist of initials, with figures against each that might represent scores for merit. Certain speculators have seen in this a list of nocturnal visits, rather like the list of Don Giovanni's conquests kept by his gleeful servant Leporello. But could it not just as well have been a list of Paris restaurants, awarding points for cuisine?

One reason for the efforts shown by these critics to establish the characteristic of homosexual promiscuity in Housman seems to be based upon his interest in pornography. Since it is known, the argument runs, that Housman read and studied pornography, must he not therefore have been sexually promiscuous? I don't believe, personally, that the two things follow at all; readers of pornography more usually have no sex life of their own, and try to enjoy other people's, vicariously.

It is true, however, that Housman read Fanny Hill, Lady Chatterley's Lover, Frank Harris' My Life and Loves, Swinburne's Whippingham Papers, and James Joyce's Ulysses. The latter he did not like, but the Swinburne he carefully annotated. In his lifetime, it will be remembered, these books were censored, and the circulation of them could involve strict penalties. But it will also be remembered, by those who have enjoyed them in our less prudish age, that they are mostly novels about sex between man and woman, and are hardly what the modern "gay" reader enthuses about.

Kate Symons, who knew him as well as any woman in his life, said that in her opinion he was too fastidious to relish the physical side of love. She was no doubt thinking about marriage; he would almost certainly have kept from her his love for Moses Jackson. But the point is well-made whether one is thinking about male or female lovers. The indications are that Housman found all physical intimacy distasteful.

To less ambivalent facts about Housman as a pleasure-seeker; it is revealing to look at the methods of transport he used. Before and during the First World War, it had to be train and ferry, obviously. But once at the starting point of his tour, he would hire a car and chauffeur. The War itself did not prevent him from travelling. He visited the Riviera in 1915, and in 1919 wrote to Grant Richards asking him to continue to use his influence to get hold of the necessary permits by whatever backdoor methods he could. But in this letter, he refers not only to the miners' strike, which he deplored, but also to his extraordinarily generous donation to the War Effort, which he regarded as private but which we shall meet again in another chapter:

…As it appears that a military permit is still required for Paris I should be glad if you could tell me whether your friend is still in power and prepared to make things easy for me. Moreover I am not clear whether, after leaving Paris for the South, one can re-enter it

Venice "on a sunshiny morning"

without further trouble. Most likely I shall not stay long in Brive or any other place, but motor about. After my sacrifices for the country during the war I am beginning to spend money on myself instead of saving it up for the Welsh miners.

The following year, however, Housman discovered the aeroplane. He was one of the earliest public figures to make use of this new-fangled invention – almost a pioneer. He wrote to Laurence in great excitement, and included a strangely prophetic afterthought:

I have just flown to Paris and back, and am never going by any other route, until they build the Channel Tunnel, which I will give a trial, if it is much cheaper.

He can hardly have anticipated that it would be another seventy-five years before any of us would have a chance to go to Paris via the Tunnel. A few weeks later he wrote to Kate describing the same experience in more detail:

Armstrong Whitworth Argosy at Croydon, the Silver Wing service, 1927

My dear Kate,

Well, I flew there, and am never going by any other route in future. Surrey from overhead is delightful, Kent and France less interesting, the Channel disappointing, because on both days there was too much mist to let both shores be seen at once. It was rather windy, and the machine sometimes imitated a ship at sea (though that is due to differing densities of atmosphere and not to wind) but not in a very lifelike manner. Members of your unhappy sex were sick, however. The noise is great, and I alighted rather deaf, not having stuffed my ears with the cotton-wool provided. Nor did I put on the lifebelt which they oblige one to take. To avoid crossing the 60 miles of sea which a straight flight would involve, they go from Croydon to Hythe, Hythe to Boulogne, Boulogne to Paris. You are in the air 2½ hours: from Leicester Square to your hotel in Paris you take little more than four; though on the return journey we were two hours late in starting because the machine required repairs, having been damaged on the previous day by a passenger who butted through the window to be sick. My chief trouble is that what I now want is no longer a motor and a chauffeur but an aeroplane and a tame pilot, which I suppose are more expensive.

As flying became more sophisticated, he kept pace with it. No doubt by 1927, when he flew over by Silver Wing, with refreshments from stewards en route, paper bags were supplied for passengers:

I flew home by the new 'Silver Wing' aeroplane, which is more roomy and steadier, and contains an attendant to supply you with cheese and biscuits and various liquors, and to point out objects of interest on the route: also an emergency door in the roof, which ought to be very tranquillising.

A far cry from the notion of the Westerly Wanderer; Housman's southern and eastern explorations by plane and car, linked as they are to high living in the best restaurants and most elegant cities of Europe, came as a great surprise to a reader like myself, who had earlier imagined only the footsore, lovesick, peasant-poet of the Shropshire Hills.

❧❧❧

CHAPTER NINE

Compassion to a painful degree

AFTER Housman the morbid recluse and Housman the self-indulgent pleasure-seeker, Housman the tenderly compassionate seems an unlikely development. The anxious solicitude which he clearly felt at times was the characteristic he most wanted to hide; Victorian manliness and modesty required that signs of ostentatious generosity must be avoided at all costs. Housman was highly self-aware; the introvert in him made him ask himself whether an act of kindness was pure, or whether it had an ulterior motive of swank. After his death his copy of The Seven Pillars of Wisdom was found to have a marginal note beside one of T. E. Lawrence's more tortured passages of self-examination: "This is me."

Writing in the Edwardian Magazine in 1936, Kate Symons put it like this:

> A. E. H. often performed quiet acts of unobtrusive generosity. Consideration for the feelings of people comfortably off he certainly had not; but, to a painful degree, he was capable of compassion for suffering, and resentment against the miseries of the world. Students of his poems find this strain in them, as, also, his admiration for those who bear hardships bravely. During the Great War he showed practical concern for his four Edwardian nephews who were with the fighting forces. On its outbreak, he sent £100 to help in equipping the three who left civilian life to join the Army; and when N. V. H. S., the youngest of them, lost his left hand, he made particular request to be allowed to supply an artificial hand to make good the loss as far as possible.

Yet publicly A. E. H. appeared wholly unmoved by the Great War, and cynical about its motives. In 1933 he wrote to Maurice Pollet:

> The Great War cannot have made much change in the opinions of any man of imagination.

At the outbreak of war in 1914, Lily Thicknesse received this ironic comment:

> …The thirst for blood is raging among the youth of England. More than half the undergraduates are away, but mostly not at the front, because they all want to be officers. I am going out when they make me a Field-Marshal. Meanwhile I have three nephews being inoculated for typhoid and catching pneumonia on Salisbury Plain and performing other acts of war calculated to make the German Emperor realise that he is a very misguided man…

One of the most enigmatic of Housman's poems, "Epitaph on an Army of Mercenaries", written in 1922 and looking back on the war, seemed both to praise the endurance of the suffering armies and to decry their concern with pay and material comfort. "Was not the whole episode pointless?" he seems to be saying, and then, "How can we survive without the earthy pragmatism of everyday men?" In recent years the correspondence columns of the Daily Telegraph have carried lengthy arguments about the true meaning of the poem:

> These, in the day when heaven was falling,
>   The hour when earth's foundations fled,
> Followed their mercenary calling
>   And took their wages and are dead.
>
> Their shoulders held the sky suspended;
>   They stood and earth's foundations stay;
> What God abandoned, these defended,
>   And saved the sum of things for pay.

All this masks an aching tenderness towards the duped and romantic young men who were, in every generation, hoodwinked into "following the colours." Very many of the poems in A Shropshire Lad take up this theme. Number XXXV is one of the best:

> On the idle hill of summer,
>   Sleepy with the flow of streams,
> Far I hear the steady drummer
>   Drumming like a noise in dreams.
>
> Far and near and low and louder
>   On the roads of earth go by,
> Dear to friends and food for powder
>   Soldiers marching, all to die.
>
> East and west on fields forgotten
>   Bleach the bones of comrades slain,
> Lovely lads and dead and rotten;
>   None that go return again.
>
> Far the calling bugles hollo,
>   High the screaming fife replies,
> Gay the files of scarlet follow:
>   Woman bore me, I will rise.

In September of 1915 there came another of those family bereavements which, like Herbert's death in 1901, touched Alfred particularly deeply. Kate's third son Clement was killed in action. This is the letter he wrote to her;

> My dear Kate,
> I have been scanning the casualty lists in these last days, and when I saw your card this morning I feared what the news must be. Well, my dear, it is little I or anyone else can do to comfort you, or think of anything to say that you will not have thought of. But I remember your telling me at the beginning of the war that he had almost a hope and expectation of dying in battle, and we must be glad that it was a victorious battle in which he died. I do not know that I can do better than to send you some verses that I wrote many years ago; because the essential business of poetry, as it has been said, is to harmonise the sadness of the universe, and it is somehow more sustaining and healing than prose. Do assure Edward of my feeling for you all, and also, though I do not know her, the poor young girl.
> Your affectionate brother,   A. E. Housman

Like "Astronomy", "Illic Jacet" was intended to describe Herbert's own motives and beliefs. But its setting is less specific and more easily applicable to the death of any young soldier; its only irony lies in the last line, for Clement, we realise, had a real sweetheart to whom he longed to return:

> Oh hard is the bed they have made him,
>   And common the blanket and cheap;
> But there he will lie as they laid him:
>   Where else could you trust him to sleep?
>
> To sleep when the bugle is crying
>   And cravens have heard and are brave,
> When mothers and sweethearts are sighing
>   And lads are in love with the grave.
>
> Oh dark is the chamber and lonely,
>   And lights and companions depart;
> But lief will he lose them and only
>   Behold the desire of his heart.
>
> And low is the roof, but it covers
>   A sleeper content to repose;
> And far from his friends and his lovers
>   He lies with the sweetheart he chose.

And here is how Kate herself described the event twenty years later:

Two of the poems that have appeared in 'The Edwardian' date from the War. They were printed in December 1915, after C. A. S. was killed in the Battle of Loos. One had been copied into an autograph book by C. A. S. just before he left England, entitled by him 'The Conflict', as it seemed to him to be the portrayal of conflict in which cowardly fear was vanquished. The other, 'Illic Jacet', was sent to me by A. E. H. after his nephew was killed. He wrote a kind letter with it saying he knew how ready C. A. S. had been to meet the death that came to him. I could tell from the letter that 'Illic Jacet' had been written some years earlier, on the death in battle of another gallant relation – our youngest brother – who was killed in the Boer War.

Perhaps the most extraordinary twist in Housman's view of the war lay in the little-known fact of his donation to the fighting funds; in response to the Chancellor's appeal in 1914 he gave the whole of his current bank balance, said to be five hundred pounds, a massive sum for those days. There was a hidden streak of sentimentality behind his view of the war. He let Grant Richards know that he wanted A Shropshire Lad to be available to every soldier, and thus cheap, for a quaint ulterior motive:

> I do not make any particular complaint about your doubling the price of my book, but of course it diminishes the sale and therefore diminishes my chances of the advertisement to which I am always looking forward: a soldier is to receive a bullet in the breast, and it is to be turned aside from his heart by a copy of A Shropshire Lad which he is carrying there. Hitherto it is only the Bible which has performed this trick.

Something like this in fact came about: A. E. H. carefully treasured a letter from an American soldier who had written to say that, in comforting a wounded British infantryman, he had offered him his copy of A Shropshire Lad. But the British soldier had responded by taking from his pocket his own bloodstained copy.

Housman's compassion extended far beyond his feelings for the common soldier. He told Basil in 1927 that he had met the American defence lawyer Clarence Darrow, and had clearly been moved, in his own ironic way, by the latter's account of criminals facing capital punishment:

> I had a visit not long ago from Clarence Darrow, the great American barrister for defending murderers. He had only a few days in England, but he could not return home without seeing me, because he had so often used my poems to rescue his clients from the electric chair. Loeb and Leopold owe their life sentence partly to me; and he gave me a copy of his speech, in which, sure enough, two of my pieces are misquoted.

The poem "Eight O'clock" from Last Poems describes in harrowing fashion the final moments of a man about to be hanged, as he hears the clock strike the hour of execution:

Katharine Symons aged 40

> He stood and heard the steeple
> > Sprinkle the quarters on the morning town.
> One, two, three, four, to market place and people
> > It tossed then down.
>
> Strapped, noosed, nighing his hour,
> > He stood and counted them and cursed his luck;
> And then the clock collected in the tower
> > Its strength and struck.

There is a personal form of tenderness which appears very seldom in Housman's letters and prose writing, but which is apparent everywhere in his verse. It is the love of the countryside, of nature, which he links with the love we feel for a special individual. The expression "achingly beautiful" is a cliché, of course; but in Housman's poems of landscape and love he does seem to ache at the beauty of it – and at the deprivation when both the landscape and the beloved are cruelly torn away. A letter in 1928 to Percy Withers gives a rare hint at how observant Housman was of nature:

> …there have been so many early springs in the last fifteen years that people have forgotten the proper time for leaves and flowers to come out. For twenty years or so from 1887 onward I noted these things in a diary, on the strength of which I inform you that the lilac usually comes into blossom on 7 May…

Two of the best-known of all his poems bring together the love of countryside and the love for a girl, "Bredon Hill" and "Is My Team Ploughing?" Anyone who has stood by the tower on the summit of Bredon, in high summer, knows exactly Housman's feeling of admiration for the English pastoral scene: the coloured counties, the larks so high, and the springing thyme. Not two but seven counties can actually be seen from this viewpoint. Housman links the beauty of this scene to the death of the storyteller's sweetheart in the snows of Christmas, and the effect is despairing.

> In summertime on Bredon
>   The bells they sound so clear;
> Round both the shires they ring them
>   In steeples far and near,
>   A happy noise to hear.
>
> Here of a Sunday morning
>   My love and I would lie,
> And see the coloured counties,
>   And hear the larks so high
>   About us in the sky.
>
> The bells would ring to call her
>   In valleys far away:
> 'Come all to church, good people;
>   Good people, come and pray.'
>   But here my love would stay.

And I would turn and answer
　　Among the springing thyme,
'Oh, peal upon our wedding,
　　And we will hear the chime,
　　And come to church in time.'

But when the snows of Christmas
　　On Bredon top were strown,
My love rose up so early
　　And stole out unbeknown
　　And went to church alone.

They tolled the one bell only,
　　Groom there was none to see,
The mourners followed after,
　　And so to church went she,
　　And would not wait for me.

The bells they sound on Bredon,
　　And still the steeples hum.
'Come all to church, good people,' -
　　Oh, noisy bells, be dumb;
　　I hear you, I will come.

In "Is My Team Ploughing?" the themes of love recur as the pairs of verses give question and answer – country, team-mates and girl. But the despair and loss belong this time to the man who has died, and the storyteller enjoys a kind of self-satisfied triumph.

"Is my team ploughing,
　　That I was used to drive
And hear the harness jingle
　　When I was man alive?"

Ay, the horses trample.
　　The harness jingles now;
No change though you lie under
　　The land you used to plough.

"Is football playing
   Along the river shore,
With lads to chase the leather,
   Now I stand up no more?"

Ay, the ball is flying,
   The lads play heart and soul;
The goal stands up, the keeper
   Stands up to keep the goal.

"Is my girl happy,
   That I thought hard to leave,
And has she tired of weeping
   As she lies down at eve?"

Ay, she lies down lightly,
She lies not down to weep:
   Your girl is well-contented.
   Be still, my lad, and sleep.

"Is my friend hearty,
Now I am thin and pine,
And has he found to sleep in
   A better bed than mine?"

Yes, lad, I lie easy,
   I lie as lads would choose;
I cheer a dead man's sweetheart,
   Never ask me whose.

The most telling and immediate compassion in Housman, however, is that which he feels for his family, for those close to him and who have in their turn shown him love and appreciation. It takes many forms, but always relates back to that sense of responsibility for his own kin which he learnt, we feel, from his dying mother. Laurence, for instance, seems for ever to have been the little brother whose literary efforts called for special supervision and encouragement. This continued in spite of the fact that he disapproved of a good deal of what

Laurence did and wrote. Laurence sent him the draft of his first book of poems, Green Arras:

> Before submitting them, I sent them to my brother Alfred for criticism; and his long critical notes which I still cherish were both kind and caustic. Thanks to him I left out several poems which I am now glad to have left out.

But in elder-brother fashion, Alfred would be careful not to overdo the praise:

> After seeing the Little Plays he said to me quite kindly, 'Not so bad as I expected,' which was as much in the direction of praise as I could have hoped to get from him.

After Alfred's death, however, Laurence made a touching discovery:

> I only sent him those of my books in which I thought he might find something to please him; but when I went through his library after his death, I found that he had got all of them in their sequent editions; that he had, in fact, got a more complete collection of my books than I had myself; and I learned from friends in Cambridge that he said kinder things about them behind my back than he did to my face.

There are many instances of generosity with his money. When Grant Richards first approached bankruptcy, Housman made him a valuable loan. When Richards wrote again, years later, in similar straits, Housman could no longer find the money:

> My dear Richards,
> It distresses me that you are once again in difficulties, the more so because this time I cannot relieve them. I am finding £450 a year for the education of a godson, and this will go on for four years. I am also involved in much expense in changing my rooms, making repairs and buying furniture, and a lift which has to be put in will cost £324.

In 1933 £450 per annum would have paid the full fees at a leading boarding school.

At the other extreme, Kate wrote to Alfred in 1929 asking whether he had an old cast-off suit that she might pass on to an elderly family gardener who was now in a bad way. Alfred did not stop at the suit, but set about equipping the old man with a virtual wardrobe:

> My dear Kate,
> Shirts had better be included; and do not stint yourself for a few shillings or indeed for more than a few. I keep my benevolence for the cases that I know about: as for distressed miners, who have twice tried to starve me, let them starve. My fear is that the suits may prove too tight. He must be restrained from writing me a nice letter.

He went so far as to thank Kate for her concern:

> My dear Kate,
> I enclose a cheque for £2 and thanks for the trouble you have taken. I hope the vests don't tickle him as most vests do me.

But typically, he himself wanted no "fuss" such as thanks. Equally typically, he had no pity for the Welsh miners, who might well be suffering grievously but who, he felt, had brought it on themselves.

One of his nephews went to Cambridge to sort out his effects after his death:

> During the inspection of A. E. H.'s possessions in his rooms, his manservant pulled down a padded aviation suit from the top of a cupboard, and my son asked if that was what his uncle wore when he used to fly to France. "Oh no," said the man,"the Professor bought that in the coal strike and used to sit writing in it to keep himself warm."

Generosity to his immediate family seems to have been, in his view, a continuous and systematic obligation. In 1907 he was concerned about Lucy's financial situation:

> My dear Laurence,
> I have induced Dr Morris to tell me, on condition that Mamma does not know that he told, the amount of his bill for last year. It is about £70 0s 0d; and I want to find out, if possible, what this will

mean to Mamma. I have no clear notion of what her income is and what margin it generally leaves her; and perhaps you or Clemence can give me some notion. I am anxious to prevent her feeling any severe pinch for the bill, but on the other hand I don't want to be extravagant or ostentatious; so if you can help me to judge what I should give her in order to effect these two ends I should be much obliged.

Twenty-two years later, here he is writing to Kate about their brother Basil, with exactly the same concern:

My dear Kate,
You will have heard from Jeannie about Basil's state of health and approaching retirement. I remember your telling me last year that you had offered to share with him what you inherited from Uncle Joe, and I suppose there is room for hope that the County Council will award him something of a pension. But as you know more of that household's affairs than I do, I wish you would tell me how much you think I ought to add in future to the £50 per annum I now send them.

When Robert died after his unheroic little accident at Iford Manor, it was Alfred who chose the inscription for the sundial that forms his monument in Smallcombe cemetery. The words could form an epitaph not merely for Robert, but for the whole of pitiful, sad, deluded humankind:

A. E. H. helped to choose the design, and he selected the inscription that runs round the base –"Our days upon the earth are as a shadow and there is none abiding."

CHAPTER TEN

ಲ್ಲ ಲ್ಲ ಲ್ಲ

The most unpleasant thing imaginable

AT THE time of Housman's death he was described by John Sparrow, himself a distinguished European scholar who became Warden of All Souls at Oxford, as the most learned Latinist in Europe. This was in an age and in a generation when the Classics were a great deal more widely taught than today, and were the automatic choice of subject for the best brains. So Sparrow's judgement was praise indeed. It is likely that Housman, if he had been so inclined, would have received honarary doctorates at half a dozen leading universities, would have been appointed to the Order of Merit, could have been knighted and might even have become Poet Laureate. But he was not so inclined. He steadfastly refused every offer of high academic honour.

As early as 1920 the University of Cambridge approached him with a request that he should consider becoming Public Orator, a sort of leading ceremonial speaker at major university functions. This was his refusal:

> Not if the stipend were £150,000 instead of £150 would I be Public Orator. I could not discharge the duties of the office without abandoning all other duties and bidding farewell to such peace of mind as I possess. You none of you have any notion what a slow and barren mind I have, nor what a trouble composition is to me (in prose, I mean: poetry is either easy or impossible.)

Was he being ironic when he described his mind as slow and barren? Could this be false modesty? It does not seem so, because a string of universities wrote to offer him an honorary Doctorate of Letters, and his refusals seem to indicate that he had thought the whole matter through, and had decided that he simply could not identify himself with this kind of preferential treatment. The most interesting of these refusals was that which he sent to Oxford:

Dear Mr Registrar,
I beg to thank you for your communication, received today, of the kind and flattering intention of the Hebdomadal Council to propose that the Degree of Doctor of Letters in the University of Oxford should be conferred upon me. My obligation to them, and my sense of the honour proposed, are not less because it is one which I am not able to accept. In pursuance of a resolution taken long ago, and for reasons which it would be tedious to enumerate and perhaps not quite easy to formulate, I have declined similar distinctions offered me by the generosity of other Universities; and the case is not altered even when the University which designs to bestow its favour on me is my own. I only ask that neither ingratitude nor lack of appreciation may be inferred from my action, as they are far indeed from my mind.
I am yours faithfully,   A. E. Housman

The same disinclination applied to his poetry. He systematically turned down applications for permission to read his poems aloud, and only Laurence was eventually able to win him over, with a request to broadcast some poems in honour of Alfred's seventieth birthday:

My dear Laurence,
Only the archangel Raphael could recite my poetry properly, but I have no doubt you would do it quite nicely, and I shall try not to set up interfering wave-lengths. But understand that I incur no obligation to do the same for you on your 70th birthday.

The eager young Houston Martin tried to persuade A. E. H. to write his autobiography, with this response:

Dear Mr Martin,
You are an engaging madman, and write more agreeably than many sane persons; but if I write anything of an autobiographical nature, as I have sometimes idly thought of doing, I shall send it to the British Museum to be kept under lock and key for fifty years.

Professor Housman in his prime

Houston Martin must rank as the most devoted of all those young soldiers who went to war with Housman in their pockets. He painted the name "A Shropshire Lad" on the tank he drove at the Normandy landings in 1944. He died as recently as 1995, an enduring personal link with the living Housman.

To all those who wished themselves to write his biography, his reply was chilling. Many there are of us who have thought long and hard before attempting such a risky undertaking. Cyril Clemens was one of the earliest:

Dear Mr Clemens,
I am naturally flattered that you should entertain the idea of writing a biography of me, but neither you nor anyone else could possibly write one and I certainly would give no assistance.

But the most remarkable of all Housman's refusals was the rejection of the Order of Merit. This of all honours one might have assumed to be acceptable to him. It is restricted to twenty-four members, of whom the greatest number have always been scholars, historians, writers, composers and artists. Two members of the Order, at least - Thomas Hardy and Robert Bridges - were poets whose work Housman genuinely admired and whom he was glad to count as friends. On the other hand, George Bernard Shaw had also refused the Order, and he was far from being someone whom Housman wanted to emulate. It is true that there were existing members whom he despised, and that the Order does extend to military grandees as well as to the creative and scholarly. There are hints both in Housman's letter of congratulation to Robert Bridges, and also in his formal refusal written to the King's private secretary, that these were valid reasons for his dislike of the Order:

> My dear Bridges,
> If the Order of Merit gives you pleasure, I shall share it; and no one can dispute your title to it. I hope you do not mind having Galsworthy for a yoke-fellow as much as I should. If ever there was a man without a spark of genius, that man is he.

The letter to Lord Stamfordham, the King's secretary, is a clear example of Housman's talent for deliberate obfuscation:

> Dear Lord Stamfordham,
> With all gratitude for His Majesty's most kind and flattering wish to confer upon me the Order of Merit I humbly beg permission to decline this high honour. I hope to escape the reproach of thanklessness or churlish behaviour by borrowing the words in which an equally loyal subject, Admiral Cornwallis, declined a similar mark of Royal favour: 'I am, unhappily, of a turn of mind that would make my receiving that honour the most unpleasant thing imaginable.'
> I am yours very truly,   A.E.Housman

Why on earth should it be the most unpleasant thing imaginable? Did he mean the Order of Merit in particular, or all honours in general?

The Great Court, Trinity College

Was it a kind of self-flagellation for earlier supposed misdemeanours, both scholastic and moral? Or did he genuinely believe that his achievements were of too low a value to justify such honour? It is bewildering; and yet, seen in the overall context of his life's work, there is a consistency in it. For Housman, knowledge and learning were ends in themselves and the acquisition of them required no pat on the back. He had spent his life in research for its own sake, and certainly believed that his achievements needed no public act of justification. In an age when modesty was manly and scholarship was an honour in itself, he had decided that he wished for no further honour.

CHAPTER ELEVEN

On the Golden Floor

HOUSMAN had written so often about death that it is unsurprising to find him pondering his own end long before it came. He did not value his own life as such, but did value his life's work. Once he could feel, in good conscience, that this was complete, the rest of his days became purely a bonus. When he took his summer holiday in 1929, with the fifth book of Manilius still incomplete, he wrote to Kate:

> …I am not flying, as I am taking great care of my life till the book I am now engaged on is finished.

But during that holiday he came face to face with real urgency, and a month later wrote to her again:

> Perhaps I had better tell you that the doctor, whom I made over-haul me when I turned 70, says that my heart is not as stout as it was and ought to be; and I found this out when climbing the Puy de Parioux, about the height of Snowdon, on a hot afternoon.

When a few months later the Manilius was ready and published, the relief in his letter to Percy Withers is palpable:

> A more cheerful piece of news is that I have just published the last book I shall ever write, and that I now mean to do nothing for ever and ever. It is one of my more serious works, so you will not read it. I am glad that there is a chance of seeing you again in Cambridge before so very long. I hope and believe that the 1908 port will last out till then.

He now had time to reassess the body of his work, and Houston Martin coaxed out of him a statement on the importance he gave to A

Shropshire Lad and Last Poems. It was an admission that the mental release of his poetry had made his life more gentle, more tolerable:

> Certainly I have never regretted the publication of my poems. The reputation which they brought, though it gives me no lively pleasure, is something like a mattress interposed between me and the hard ground.

But in 1933 he had been taken seriously ill during his summer holiday on the Loire, and wrote to Kate from Blois:

> ...I had two days of the most violent and frequent pain I have ever undergone, though that may only mean that hitherto I have been more fortunate than most people. I could not swallow a morsel of food or a drop to drink without such pain as made me fear to repeat the action; and I could not get three minutes sleep at a time because the phlegm collected and started a spasm.

Back at Cambridge he was admitted to the Evelyn Nursing Home, the first of a series of such admissions, with heart trouble. The first visit did not last for long, but by 1935 he was having great breathing difficulties, which made lengthy sleep almost impossible. He recognised in himself the Cheyne-Stokes respiration which he had read of in Arnold Bennett's Clayhanger. Now it became apparent that walking long distances in the country had been, after all, a real pleasure to him; but it was a delight lost forever:

> The doctor does not want me to take walks of much more than a mile, and I myself am often inclined not to do much more than twice that amount. I still go up my 44 stairs two at a time, but that is in the hopes of dropping dead at the top.

But he did not drop dead, and the Fellows decided to move him out of his bleak and austere quarters in Whewell's Court and into the main buildings of Trinity. He was offered ground floor rooms in a corner of the Great Court. His friend and colleague A.S.F.Gow supervised the move. Housman was in a state of great nervous tension about this, but still found his old enthusiasm for the scientifically new-fangled, writing to Kate:

AEH aged 75, with his great-nephew Michael Symons, in 1934

My new rooms are much admired, especially as to bathroom and lavatory, by those who have properly examined them, and are said to be the last word in luxurious and scientific plumbing. Did you ever hear of a thermostat ? a thing which watches the thermometer and sends the temperature up when it begins to fall.

The premonition of death brought some self-examination, so that several letters of this time give a precise insight into Housman's religious stand. To Maurice Pollet in 1933 he wrote:

I was brought up in the Church of England and in the High Church party, which is much the best religion I have ever come across. But Lempriere's Classical Dictionary, which fell into my hands when I was eight, attached my affections to paganism. I became a deist at thirteen and an atheist at twenty-one.

Nothing in his experience after the age of twenty-one altered that view. His personal disasters – his mother's death, Oxford, Moses Jackson – and the early deaths of several of his close family, can only have confirmed his reluctance to recognise any divine benevolence. As an interesting footnote, in the same letter to Maurice Pollet he wrote, "Oxford had not much effect on me, except that there I met my greatest friend."

To Houston Martin he repeated his favourite résumé of his attitude to life:

In philosophy I am a Cyrenaic or egoistic hedonist, and regard the pleasures of the moment as the only possible motive of action. As for pessimism, I think it almost as silly, though not as wicked, as optimism. George Eliot said she was a meliorist: I am a pejorist, and also yours sincerely,   A. E. Housman

George Eliot's "meliorism" seems to imply a belief that human life may tend to improve, provided that human effort strives towards this goal. Housman's "pejorism" means the reverse: that is, things will get comparatively worse. But this piece of grammatical pedantry was Housman's way of teasing his young admirer. To Kate, however, who wrote to say that she was praying for his recovery, his reply was more simple and sincere:

I abandoned Christianity at thirteen but went on believing in God till I was twenty-one, and towards the end of that time I did a good deal of praying for certain persons and myself. I cannot help being touched that you do it for me, and feeling rather remorseful, because it must be an expenditure of energy, and I cannot believe in its efficacy.

Five months later, in April 1936, his doctor admitted him to the

Evelyn Nursing Home for the final time. His last correspondence was a post card to Kate:

Back to Evelyn nursing home to-day (Saturday).
Ugh.   A. E. H.

His last recorded words, however, are humorous ones, given by Laurence, who received a letter from the doctor describing A. E. H.'s last hours:

"You know," he said, "how silent and reserved he always was; but this time he talked quite a lot, and very affectionately. He held my hand for nearly half an hour. "You have been a good friend to me," he said. "I know you have brought me here so that I may not commit suicide, and I know that you may not help me to do it more than the Law allows. But I do ask you not to let me have any more unnecessary suffering than you can help." I told him that he should not suffer any more; and from that time on he did not. Then, to cheer him just before I left, I told him a thoroughly naughty story. He was very weak, but he threw back his head on the pillow, laughing heartily. "That's a good one," he said, "and tomorrow I shall be telling it again on the Golden Floor."

He was as precise as ever. The next day, he died. At his funeral in Trinity College Chapel, his own hymn, "For My Funeral", was sung:

> O thou that from thy mansion,
> > Through time and place to roam,
> Dost send abroad thy children,
> > And then dost call them home,
>
> That men and tribes and nations
> > And all thy hand hath made
> May shelter them from sunshine
> > In thine eternal shade:
>
> We now to peace and darkness
> > And earth and thee restore
> Thy creature that thou madest
> > And wilt cast forth no more.

Enigmatically beautiful as ever, it suggests a divine presence to those who want to find it there, but a mere return of dust to dust, to those who look for no other point in life.

His ashes were taken to Ludlow Church, which reminds us that A Shropshire Lad is, when all is said and done, that part of his life's work which has given the greatest pleasure to the greatest number. The plaque on the wall bears the first three lines of "Parta Quies", most tender of all his poems, which he had written as an undergraduate at St John's fifty-six years before:

> Goodnight; ensured release,
>   Imperishable peace,
> Have these for yours,
>   While sea abides, and land,
> And earth's foundations stand,
>   And heaven endures.
>
> When earth's foundations flee,
>   Nor sky nor land nor sea
> At all is found,
>   Content you, let them burn:
> It is not your concern;
>   Sleep on, sleep sound.

Now that Housman has gone to tell his tale upon the Golden Floor, a legion of critics, analysts, biographers and anthologists have attempted to summarise his character and his work. It is well-nigh impossible. A man so rich in variety, so full of antitheses, so abstruse in his learning and so moving in his sentiment cannot be briefly summarised. The best one can attempt is a presentation of the main contrasts in his character, together with a quotation from his own introduction to Manilius:

> If a man will comprehend the richness and variety of the universe, and inspire his mind with a due measure of wonder and of awe, he must contemplate the human intellect not only on its heights of genius but in its abysses of ineptitude...

Housman had the mind of the most learned Latinist in Europe, but the heart of a remorseful and bewildered lover. He was an insistent atheist, yet lost in wonder at the universe. He was ascetically rigorous in his work and his personal habits, yet he described himself as a hedonist, and knew food, wine, city life and pornography like a latter-day Silenus. He understood nature and the simple life, the pastoral beauty of western England and the pleasure of country rambling close to the wild; yet he was familiar with the greatest architecture and literature of the civilised world. He was self-centred and, when not dourly silent, unpardonably rude, yet to some he was generous to a fault and a merry companion. He gave no quarter in his harsh professional criticism, and expected none in return; yet he was modest to the extent of refusing every kind of honour and adulation. He was a homosexual, who inspired countless young men with love for their girlfriends.

Where in all this lies the Westerly Wanderer? He is always there, sometimes hidden, sometimes denied, but there in the man's longest memories and deepest yearnings. Housman did wander in the West of his nostalgic dreams, did in the end know those places, from personally tramping the footpaths, woods and pasture slopes of South Shropshire. But mostly the Westerly Wanderer lay in his memory and his heart – those parts of his richness and variety which he most wanted to hide from us, but which we have loved the most.

Two contrasting Cambridge acquaintances have left contrasting memories of Housman. To Enoch Powell, it was the self-motivated and self-controlled scholar who counted most:

Courage, moral and intellectual, was what Housman came to represent to me in the two years during which I sat at his feet in the lecture room and the single year – it was no more – during which we dined at the same High Table.

Housman's college servant – his bedmaker – saw instead the humanity of the man. To Laurence he said:

I loved your brother. When I first began to do for him, I used to be afraid to go into the room. But it was all right, when I got to know him.

That, it seems to me, will do perfectly well, for a summary of Alfred Edward Housman: We loved him; we were afraid of him; but it was all right, when we got to know him.

ﮩﮩﮩﮩ

Further reading

A select list of the more recent publications.

Graves, Richard Perceval   A. E. Housman: The Scholar-Poet
Oxford University Press 1981

Page, Norman   A.E.Housman: A Critical Biography
New York 1983

Ricks, Christopher   Collected Poems and Selected Prose
Allen Lane 1988

Naiditch, P.G.   A. E .Housman, in Classical Scholarship,
A Biographical Encyclopaedia,
Ed. Briggs and Calder.   *Garland 1990*

Jebb, Keith   A. E. Housman
Seren Books 1992

Shaw, Robin   Housman's Places. A guide.
The Housman Society 1995

Birch, J.Roy (editor)   Unkind to Unicorns: Selected Comic Verse
The Housman Society & Silent Books 1995

Burnett, Archie   The Collected Verse of A.E.Housman
Oxford University Press 1996

Sources used for quotation:

Maas, Henry   The Letters of A.E.Housman
Hart Davis 1971

Symons, Mrs E.W. (Kate) Memories of A. E Housman
More Memories of A.E.H.
King Edwards School, Bath 1936
Alfred Edward Housman: Recollections
New York 1937

Housman, Laurence   The Unexpected Years
A. E. H. A Memoir
London 1937

Excerpts:

I	The West
XII	The laws of God, the laws of man
XXIV	Epithalamium

From More Poems, published by Laurence Housman after A. E. H.'s death

XXII	I promise nothing; friends will part
XLVII	For my Funeral
XLVIII	Parta Quies

Excerpt:

XLII	A. J. J.

From Additional Poems, also published by Laurence Housman

VII	He would not stay for me; and who can wonder?
XVIII	Oh who is that young sinner with the handcuffs on his wrists?

From unpublished comic verse

My Dear Mamma I cannot say
Hallelujah Hannah
Hallelujah was the only observation
At the door of my own little hovel